SIMONE WEIL:
AN INTRODUCTION

Other Works in
The Pennbridge Introductory Series

Adorno   by Willem van Reijen
Foucault   by Hinrich Fink-Eitel
Habermas   by Detlef Horster

SIMONE WEIL: AN INTRODUCTION

Heinz Abosch

Translated from the German
by Kimberly A. Kenny

Pennbridge Books
New York

ADVISORY BOARD

Professor Detlef Horster, Ph.D.
Professor Ekkehard Martens, Ph.D.
Professor Herbert Schnädelbach, Ph.D.
Professor Ralf Schnell, Ph.D.
Professor Alfred Schöpf, Ph.D.
Prof. Jörg Zimmermann, Ph.D.

Pennbridge Books, April 1994
Translation copyright © 1993 by Pennbridge Communications Inc.

Library of Congress Catalog Card Number
94-066247

Design: Falco & Falco Inc.
Typesetting: MacLean & Tuminelly
Printing: Versa Press Inc.

Manufactured in the United States
ISBN 1-880055-03-1

CONTENTS

"Human relationships must be relegated to the category of unmeasurable things. It should be openly recognized that a miner, a printer, a minister are the same."

—Simone Weil

INTRODUCTION

The brief life of Simone Weil was filled with intellectual drama. Yet, when she died in 1943 at the age of 34, few had taken notice of her life. The greater part of her writings appeared posthumously and were heavily edited because editors did not believe they were worthy of publication in their entirety. This made it difficult to comprehend the thinking of this French philosopher, her development, and her motives and goals.

Above all, research was made difficult by the division of her intellectual development into two distinguishable phases each lasting approximately five years: the phase of revolutionary reflection from 1931 to 1936 and the phase of religious reflection from 1938 to 1943. As a result of this division, the picture of her work presented to the public was extremely fragmented. Texts from the last years of her life became famous, while those from the beginning of her life were ignored. With the appearance of additional publications, this situation slowly changed and it gradually became possible to survey the development of Simone Weil's thought. We must wait to see whether the newly begun edition of her collected works will reveal additional important insights.

Hardly famous during the course of her life, Simone Weil acquired a posthumous fame which increased from year to year and may not yet have reached its zenith. An impressive number of portrayals, scholarly and popular, apologetic and critical, have appeared. Interest became most evident in France where her work was first published with Albert Camus as the editor. Since then her fame has spread to other countries including America and Japan. Her dramatic figure attracted the television medium and, finally, the philosopher was even celebrated as a theatrical heroine and honored as "a saint." There were high-flown comparisons, in colorful combination and not always in good taste, to Antigone, the Maid of Orleans and Rosa Luxemburg.

The promise of the pensive and the provoking presents a challenge to those who study her. It is not at all surprising that this life provides a rare fascination. As a philosopher, Simone Weil distinguished herself from all others in her field. Years before Sartre she practiced "engagement," wrote theoretical treatises and political manifestos, taught philosophy and fought as a revolutionary, meditated and worked in a metal factory. Ultimately, she abandoned rational thought in favor of religious mysticism. At the same time despairing and happy, she sought and found death.

Such explosively unusual characteristics explain her influence on people of the most diverse convictions and their differing perceptions of her. While some are interested in her intellectual substance, others enjoy the spectacular drama, the surprising gestures, the escape from the banal. Indeed, the enjoyment of the spectacle goes beyond the subject itself.

This factor led Raymond Aron, a fellow student, to uncharacteristic reserve when reviewing her work. "I hesitate to write something about Simone Weil because this extraordinary woman has become a cult figure," he said. "Any remark which is not exclusively admiring, which she certainly deserves, threatens to be shocking, disillusioning."[1] For personal reasons such an attitude might be understandable, yet one cannot endorse it.

Conscious of the lurking dangers, emotions will be avoided here whenever possible. The intention of this work is neither to encourage a cult nor an anti-cult, but rather to examine the problems of an intellectual life. There are a number of stumbling blocks to be avoided. Besides the emotional temptation, there is the difficulty of comprehending a life composed of two halves— one revolutionary and one religious. Each of these pieces of Simone Weil's personality must be recognized for its uniqueness. At the same time, one must be aware of the connecting threads which hold everything together. As much as the two phases of her life differ from one another, they are not separated hermetically. Certain perceptions and attitudes are consistent. Beginnings of religious faith are found in the soul of this revolutionary, while, similarly, the mystic later came to profess ideas of an anarchistic nature.

As expected, the rapturous, idealizing biographies provoked intense reactions. In this vein, Jean Améry provided the most outspoken testimony. Condemning Simone Weil across the board, he warned "against an influence which cannot engender anything good" because those ideas are a "nostalgic utopia...longing for the historically decrepit." His tirade ended with this scathing judgement: "As a thinker, she has no bearing on anyone whose subject is the education of humankind."[2] Améry rebelled against the "Simone Weil myth" yet in his excessive anger he failed to recognize achievement and rejected ideas which were less nostalgic than progressive. Moreover, he remained loyal to an ideological tenet whose weakness the French philosopher had proven incontrovertibly.

The following essay will not silence criticism, rather criticism will unfold on a firmer foundation. Emotionally charged homages as well as virulent accusations will be avoided. Defending Simone Weil against some of her defenders is quite unavoidable. This does not apply only to those who obscure her declarations—largely with clouds of incense—but also to those academic assessments which often amount to a distortion of Weil's work. As valuable as scholarly research might be, a thought is altered when its intimate relation to practice falls from view.

Simone Weil was both theoretician and practitioner. Her intellect was impelled to action and there found its crowning achievement. Whoever ignores this fact misses the substance of her work. Her first biographers, Jean-Marie Perrin and Gustave Thibon, realized early the vexation of the cult of euphoria, although they themselves contributed to this movement with a heavily "Catholic interpretation." They stated, "Simone Weil has become a star of heroism and the spirit of sacrifice—with all of the artifice and speciousness that the concept entails."[3]

This examination, however, will not pay homage to a cult object, rather it will analyze the development of a philosophy. We employ an historical method to portray a life and an evolving thought process which was determined decisively by political events—Hitler's dictatorship, the Spanish Civil War, and the Second World War.

Simone Weil's criticism of an unchecked industrial system which oppresses human beings, plunders natural resources, and harms the environment, has shown itself to be valid even today. The collapse of the communist system substantiates important analyses of this French thinker. After a half century, her analyses have lost the mystique which at that time dazed naive believers.

At a time in which socialist doctrines are shaken, Simone Weil has something essential to convey. She emphasized that the actual rights of the employed were what was critical, not the ownership ratios of production capabilities, whether privately or state-owned. The way from Karl Marx to Simone Weil could be a continuum, thrust through a long, disappointing historical experience.

1

EARLY REVOLT

A born rebel, Simone Weil exhibited signs of an outsider as a child, protesting against prevalent views and prohibitions. Born into a secure economic environment, her father was a reputable physician, she was loved dearly by her parents and her brother, André, three years her senior. According to her own account, she was "raised in total agnosticism" and "never took the slightest effort to move beyond it." Her parents were French Jews, free-thinkers and democrats. Such a broad world-view from supporters of the Republic was not unusual within the Parisian bourgeois. Nothing in her family structure forecast rebellion. Yet by the age of ten she was characterizing herself as a Bolshevik and putting the symbol of the hammer and sickle on her school notebooks.

This early protest against her milieu and its ideas was not taken seriously. "As a child she was disposed toward provocative jokes *pour épater les bourgeois*," writes Athanasioa Moulakis who viewed this behavior as "typical student joking."[4] Even in later years, her parents spoke about the "student jokes" and André nicknamed his sister after a legendary Scandinavian figure, calling her "a troll," a gremlin who is always in the mood for surprising tricks.

But this characterization describes only the appearance of her early behavior, not the reality of its implications. These were not pranks, but rather expressions of a view of life which clearly distinguished itself from that of other people in many respects. The customary protest of youth is, as a rule, perfunctory, and comes to an end with adulthood. It was otherwise for Simone Weil who reached a decision which remained in force for her entire life—to protest against generally sanctioned norms, against established injustice.

Her thinking was in accord with Brecht's conception in *The Exception and the Rule:*

> What is the rule, recognize it as an abuse
> And where you have recognized abuse
> Do something about it!

Simone Weil's upbringing provided an example of this type of activity. Her mother protested against the way in which femininity was typically promoted in child rearing. "I do my best," said her mother about the five-year-old, "to develop not the charm of a girl, but rather the straightforwardness of a boy, even if this might resemble abruptness."[5]

The consequences of this action were evident—Simone Weil engaged in masculine behavior. An attractive young girl, she dressed in a consciously inelegant way in an effort to conceal her beauty. As a student, her apparel consisted of flat shoes, wool stockings, a dress, a beret, a rough overcoat with wide pockets full of newspapers with the communistic *L'Humanité* prominently displayed. There were only four female students in the philosophy classes of her teacher, Alain, and she wanted to compete directly with the men. As an expression of her emancipation she smoked cigarettes and played the decidedly masculine sport of rugby, a sport whose demands were in no way compatible with her physical weakness. In the winter of 1930, she contracted a stubborn ear infection and her constant headaches, which had been going on for some time, worsened. Ultimately, her imitation of masculine behavior was not as much of a motivation as her admiration for her brother André, a highly gifted mathematician who successfully completed his studies easily and at an indescribably rapid pace. The successes of her envied brother plunged Simone Weil into unfathomable despair. When at sixteen years old her brother was accepted to the Ecole Normale Supérieure with distinction she wanted to die:

> At the age of fourteen, I fell into one of those boundless despairing times of youth and I seriously thought about dying because of my insufficient intellectual abilities. My brother's extraordinary gift, evident at a time when his youth was comparable to Pascal's, forced me to be aware of my own shortcomings. I envied him not for the sake of outward successes, but rather regretted not being able to hope to enter that transcendental kingdom, to which only the really great human beings find admission—there, where truth is.[6]

Here an uncommon ambition reveals itself, a will reaching beyond the average; for Simone Weil was herself an excellent student, always among the best, and the favorite pupil of her philosophy teacher, Alain.

Due to the self-confidence of this child, her upbringing was not easy. Simone Weil had a frail constitution and was frequently sick. When she was twelve she began to have severe headaches which never stopped, and which later became unbearable. In addition, there was her aversion to eating which required constant, unbearable monitoring. "Eating was more of an effort than a pleasure for her," reports a childhood friend, Simone Pétrement.[7]

Such difficulties with the nourishment of a child are generally attributed to a troubled relationship with the mother. The mother is the first to provide nourishment to the child, and symbolically she never stops doing so. In this matter, Simone Weil's father, gentle and reserved, happily yielded.

Her mother did not. She was extremely loving, but had a great ability to get her own way. Simone Petrément gives the following portrait of Salomea Weil:

> In conversation she was as amusing as she was wise. She knew how to convince with so much fervor and charm, that one was defenseless against it. Very generous, she dedicated herself unreservedly to her family and friends. She made unending plans for them, advised, helped, worked tirelessly. The strength of her affection, like the strength of her organizational talent, was so great, that one was tempted, to submit oneself to her, to let oneself be guided.[8]

The relationship between this loving, clever, strong-willed mother and her daughter, was close, trusting, and warm. Yet the superior strength of the mother occasionally evoked resistance, often subliminal, though sometimes to the point of open opposition.

The first opposition must have manifested itself in the area of eating. If one listens to the psychologists, there is no doubt in this regard. As Anna Freud writes: "The child is always inclined to treat the food given by the mother as it treats the mother herself. This means that the whole abundance of potential problems in the mother-child relationship can penetrate the eating sphere. In the course of its development, the child experiences many negative effects of anger, jealousy and resentment towards the mother, which at times are displaced onto the food."[9]

One can probably apply this analysis in the case being discussed here. Relations between Simone Weil and her mother remained warm, but in the depths of her heart and soul estrangement was growing. Gestures of protest later revealed themselves very clearly. Concealing her intimate thoughts, Simone tried frequently to escape her mother's proximity. Inadequate nourishment caused leanness which again suited her wish to assimilate into a masculine body.

On that subject, Simone Petrément states: "One must assume that she made the decision to be as masculine as possible. This decision might have appeared childish if it had not been tied to certain deeply-held aspirations."[10] Her beauty, hidden for the time being, was eventually permanently damaged. Ugliness rather than beauty represented the ideal. Later it was unimaginable to her that someone could feel friendship for her. Her increasingly strong aversion to food caused a mania for thinness, in medical terms, anorexia, which often leads to death—an applicable course of the disease for Simone Weil.

Non-conformism was not unusual among the student youth of the Twenties; the examples of Sartre, Simone de Beauvoir, André Breton, Louis Aragon, Emmanuel Mounier, Paul Nizan and Claude Levi-Strauss demonstrate this. But Simone Weil's behavior distinguished itself in its peculiarities by greater determination, zest for action, even desire for provocation.

She did not try to adapt to circumstances, but instead envisioned rebellion against them. Professional failure was not only accepted, but directly sought as an accomplishment. "I have always imagined my dismissal [from her teaching position] as the crowning point of my career," she said. In this connection, words were not sufficient for Simone Weil. Her sense of conviction desired action, was impelled toward it in order to manifest itself visibly. Intent on results, Simone Weil's thinking tended not toward appeasement, but rather toward sharp alternatives. This repelled quite a few and it was difficult to be on good terms with the rigid prophet. Simone Petrément remarks:

> Actually, she was a mix of coldness and passion. On the one hand, deliberate, austere, composed and slow; on the other hand, lively, with sometimes clumsy, sometimes naively charming gestures, a fire of enthusiasm, intense indignation. In her sentimentality it could also be seen that she was dif-

ferent from the majority. This was true, above all, because to
a rare extent she seemed to forget every personal interest or
desire. She was enthused about noble issues, but without
regard to herself. Her vehemence was reserved only for the
common welfare and for the truth.

In a certain sense, she was very proud, but she was not vain,
allowing blows to her ego to go unattended, and even
approaching those who did not like her. She seemed to be
without vengeance, and without anger in those things which
affected her alone. She did not think about pleasing others
and accordingly showed no timidity in dealings with her comrades. Even her awkwardness seemed to come from the fact
that she was not composed of our coarse matter. She distinguished herself by virtue of her noble feelings and her
strengths of character, more so than due to her intelligence—
by being above average.[11]

When first meeting her, a certain amount of time was
required until the ice broke and her inner self was found. Not
without uneasiness, a fellow student remembered: "She
demonstrated total non-conformity in questions of fashion
and extremism in politics, which, given her youth, had something affected about it."

Even Raymond Aron, who admired her first essays, states:
"It seemed to me that intellectual intercourse with Simone
was almost impossible. She was notoriously without doubt;
even when her opinions changed, she was nonetheless categorical."[12] It was always all or nothing with no room for half-
measures. This scathingly sharp either/or did not allow for
tolerance. Simone de Beauvoir, a student at the same institute
at the same time, reports that she was interested in her fellow
student "because of the great reputation for cleverness that
she enjoyed, and because of her bizarre figure."

A great famine had ravaged China, and I was told that she
broke into sobs at the announcement of this news. These
tears compelled more respect from me than did her talent for

philosophy. I envied her a heart which was capable of beating
for the entire universe. One day I succeeded in making her
acquaintance. I do not know how it was that we came to speak
to each other. She explained in a sharp tone that only one
thing in the world counts today—a revolution which would
give all people food to eat. In a no less peremptory manner, I
objected to that saying that the problem consists not of
making people happy, but rather of finding sense in their lives.
She fixed me with a look. "One sees that you have never suffered from starvation," she said. With that our relationship
was already at an end.[13]

Evident here is Simone Weil's peculiarity, the radicalness
of her viewpoint distinguished her from the majority of serious students. Intellectual problems acquire existential meaning; thought does not remain in the theoretical sphere; it
craves practical realization. Her pronunciation had peculiarities which reminded one of a foreigner. Her manner of speak-
ing was slow, in an even tone, never excited, demonstrating
great self-control. Her handwriting revealed this same calm,
it was rounded and uniform, somewhat childish. Her work
was almost without revisions, written in one torrent.

Her first energetic opposition was directed against the
colonial system which Simone Weil perceived as a personal
affront. The scope of her thinking was not national but international, comprising the whole world. In this feeling of community with all peoples, she was enthusiastic about the
Russian and Chinese Revolution and supported the struggle
of the German left against Hitler. Her rejection of Nationalism
was vehement and more passionate than the majority of non-
conformist students who, despite their opposition, did not
question its relevance for French society. Simone Weil acted
without regard to the dictates of caution and stressed her
internationalist conviction. In searching for the motives for
her behavior, one must remember her family circumstances.

Because of their fragile, always precarious integration
into the political system of which they were citizens, Jews

were inclined to defend the cosmopolitan position against Nationalism. There are numerous examples of this, from Marx to Rosa Luxemburg to Trotsky.

Simone Weil's parents were non-religious Jews. Her father came from Alsace, her mother, from Russia. Their daughter was raised as an agnostic. Judaism represented something foreign to her; furthermore, she sought to escape from it. Her conversion to Christianity occurred within the context of anti-Jewish omens. She felt solidarity with the persecuted, however, the persecution of the Jews, which in its horror exceeded all others, was ignored.

In a letter from 1941 to Xavier Vallat, the Deputy for Jewish Affairs, in which she sought reinstatement to the teaching profession from which the racial laws had excluded her, Simone Weil emphasized: "I have no affection for the Jewish religion, no connection with the Jewish tradition. Since earliest childhood, I have been molded by Hellenic, Christian and French traditions."[14]

This is indisputable, yet at issue are her efforts to repress some facts, while seeking to overplay others. The repression is all the more assiduous as it attempts to ignore uncontrovertible facts. What should not be true, must not be true. Freud calls this behavior "irrational, magical nature." Thereby, one wants "to revoke the past itself, repress it voluntarily or through the involuntary repetition of the counteraction of a surfacing, tabooed thought, render it *undone*."[15] Such assiduous attempts at repression manifested themselves in Simone Weil with increasing intensity.

What she denied was nonetheless present. Judaism was in no respect as absent as she portrayed it. Even in an agnostic family like the Weils, it was no secret. In 1909, the year of Simone's birth, the Dreyfus Affair, which had stirred up France and alarmed the Jewish element of the population, was just dying down, but not yet forgotten. The consequences remained in evidence; the memory of it, fresh. In

Marcel Proust's novel, *Remembrance of Things Past*, written the year after the event—the Dreyfus Affair is portrayed as the most important, socio-political conflict of the time.

One must assume that the family of Doctor Bernard Weil was affected by it to some extent. Even if one wanted to ignore the incident, it was present and had its effects. That Simone Weil's parents, who took an active part in all events, did not speak about the Dreyfus Affair is implausible given that totally disinterested parties were expressing their views about it. Jews felt themselves threatened by the anti-semitic campaign. This particularly applied to Doctor Weil and his wife since they stood to the left politically and were in no way politically indifferent. The outbreaks of hate that resulted from the Dreyfus Affair reminded the Jews, including the Weils, that even when they were well-assimilated they occupied a special, precarious position.

Moreover, Jewish heritage was obtained through the grandparents, who were more closely associated with the tradition. Originally her mother's family had come from Eastern Europe, this created connections beyond the French border. The tradition of the imprisoned Eastern Jewry, with the contribution of its specific spirit, was prevalent. This invokes a previous point: that the rebellious daughter naturally thought not in narrowly national terms, but in universal terms. She quickly felt at home in other countries and in conversation with people of other nationalities she felt no unfamiliarity. With the French intellectuals of her generation it was otherwise. Even the extremists to the left were more likely nationally inclined; they believed more strongly about matters within the borders of their country.

The Jewish heritage that Simone Weil rejected was part of her own intellectual make-up. In his book, Paul Giniewski attributes this to "self-hatred"—a phenomenon which occurs in the case of some Jews, from Karl Marx to Karl Kraus. Those affected adapt to their environment and adopt the prevailing prejudices. Giniewski writes: "Simone Weil was interested neither in the whole of humankind nor in equal justice for all, but rather in justice for only a few of her own choosing." Jews remained excluded from her past, present and future. In 1936, as tears of shame choked her because white masters maimed or kicked Vietnamese workers to death, defenseless Jews had been worked to death in German concentration camps for three years. The newspapers reported both events. Yet the murdered Jews did not move her to tears, nor did they hinder her food intake. This is quite meaningful.[16]

Simone Weil ignored the persecution and extermination of the Jews until the end of her life. This severe charge cannot be dismissed; it is substantiated by numerous other grave, inexplicable facts. Furthermore, in her darkest period, she wrote loathsome, anti-Jewish texts. Athanasios Moulakis cautions that Simone Weil considered factory labor an unbearable malediction, while not perceiving the horror of the racism. "Even if Simone Weil might not have been in possession of the details about Oranienburg and Dachau, which, in contrast to other not easily available information, she never tried to procure for herself, her ambivalence toward the persecution of Jews remains astonishing for a human being who put misery at the center of her thinking. The misery of the century is not the factory, but the gas chamber."[17]

Such dismaying behavior, which defies rational explanation, suggests unconscious emotional disturbances which manifested themselves all the more strongly as the attempt was made to suppress them. Emmanuel Levinas and Paul Giniewski accuse the philosopher of the betrayal of Judaism, this charge is partially justified, but not completely. One can only betray that in which one has believed. Simone Weil was never a believing Jew, she always lived outside of the faith. Yet, in a broader sense this charge holds true—her turning away from the persecuted Jews was an abandonment of the principle of human solidarity. We are forced to accept that this rejection of Judaism is a disappointing aspect of Simone Weil's activism.

As we have seen, she repudiated all that was imposed upon her: prevailing ideas, bourgeois existence, and the traditional role of women. Judaism, this traditional heritage with its persistent demands, received the same treatment. This rebellious woman reacted to it with her usual indignation. This might explain one motive for her attitude, although it certainly does not explain the extreme forms of delusion in which she engaged.

Despite her denials, the rejected heritage was present. One finds it in her constant effort to translate thought into social action, to realize justice here and now. Nowhere is there a more valid analogy to this unceasing effort to reconcile thought and deed than in the Israeli agricultural settlements which are related to some of Simone Weil's ideas. Her thought had a universal, markedly non-nationalistic dimension. This was characteristic of the Jewish thinkers of the Enlightenment. Less attracted to nationalism, they were generally its resolved enemies. In this sense, Simone Weil's origins reveal themselves. This also becomes clear in her passionate, clearly obsessive concentration on the intellectual, which scarcely tolerated diversion or relaxation. To be sure she could enjoy sports, nature and music, but only in limited measure. Her intellect always had the upper hand, translating experience into theoretical concepts.

Her interpretation of Christianity also features Jewish aspects. At the center of her design stood the one God, for which Christ was its model. This corresponded more to Protestantism than to Catholicism—which this philosopher evidently never perceived. In her faith there was no room for the multitude of Catholic saints. According to Robert Coles: "This type of faith—an existentialism of a particular and demanding sort—brings her more to the vicinity of

Kirkegaard than Pascal; an existentialism more Protestant than Catholic."[18] Maja Wicki-Vogt presents her reflections under the heading, "Jewish thought in disavowed tradition."[19] That Simone Weil suppressed this tradition was indeed a "defect," Author Wicki-Vogt concedes. On the other hand, she notes, "In order to demonstrate Simone Weil's 'implicit' Jewishness, it would suffice to establish her nearness to the spirit of the Bible from which she draws as can only be done from one's own patrimony." The social ideal of justice, as the prophets proclaimed it, is unmistakable. Unmistakable also, is the hidden, invisible God of the Bible. Yet with Simone Weil there is no coup de grace, but rather a diffuse echo, which is never named, concealed by constant repression.

This overwhelmingly intellectual persona, focused on one single goal, often produced a strange effect, making close contact with others difficult. Simone Pétrement remembers her this way:

> Small, narrow face almost covered by hair and glasses. Finely-formed nose, black eyes with a bold glance. A neck, which stretched forwards, giving the impression of a passionate, insistent curiosity. But the mouth, with its full lips, expressed gentleness and goodness. If one looked carefully, her features were not lacking in grace and even beauty. It was, at the same time, a gentle countenance, boldly inquisitive, yet with a shy smile which seemed amused with itself. Now was it the thick glasses or her expression, always examining, knowing, wanting to judge? The charm remained hidden from most people who, in Simone Weil, saw only a purely intellectual creature. A delicate body, lively, but mostly awkward gestures...All of this formed a strange figure, who recalled the revolutionary intelligentsia, and, for whatever reason, completely exasperated some people. This is true even today.[20]

A fellow female student in Alain's philosophy class reports that even the teacher, who soon esteemed Simone Weil, at first felt "a basic mistrust towards a character so little earth-bound and so strange. His early judgement was influenced perhaps a little by the first impression that Simone Weil made on many people—that she lacked an element common to all human beings, a natural substance so to speak."[21] This is a reproach of an almost stereotypical sort, which Jewish thinkers often encountered and which, in a perverse manner, emphasized the anti-semitic vocabulary.

In spite of her zealous effort to free herself from it, Judaism clung to Simone Weil. Her rebellion was that of a "pariah," from the example of the Jewish intellectual, as Hannah Arendt has portrayed it. In bourgeois society, Jews were to have the choice between the parvenu and the pariah, between the upstart and the outsider.[22] The parvenu seeks to bring about his social acceptance through assimilation, while the pariah accepts his uniqueness so that he "can behold life as a whole." But neither one of them can escape his origins. For the parvenu Rahel Varnhagen, as for the pariah Simone Weil, Hannah Arendt's judgement holds true: "One cannot extricate oneself from Judaism." As a revolutionary, Simone Weil consciously chose the position of the pariah; later, as a theologian, she tried to assimilate herself to Christianity. This was all in vain. She remained a pariah, an outsider, an outcast.

Consequently, she never stopped giving expression to a feeling of alienation and isolation. She rebelled against all existing relations—against the State, against society, against her personal existence as a member of her class. She rebelled against existing definitions—as a woman, as an intellectual, as a Jew and as a Frenchwoman. Ultimately, she rejected life completely and chose death. Perceiving all of her circumstances as a limitation, she worked to overcome them. One of the most complete subversives, she denied all things traditional, one after the other.

The protest against her parents, to whom she was nevertheless bound by sincere affection, was included in this revolt. But the divergences were becoming more evident as her parents also embodied that which their daughter rejected. Again and again she took flight and again and again she returned. Not until the end of her life did she carry out the separation—in order to die. She had hidden her most intimate thoughts, her religious reflections, from her parents. She concealed the reality of her last weeks of life by means of false accounts. Thus their formerly close relationship ended in complete falsehood.

2

MASTER ALAIN

The teacher who exercised the most enduring influence on Simone Weil was Emile Auguste Chartier, famous under the pseudonym Alain. For three years, from 1925 to 1928, she took part in his philosophy classes at the renown Lycée Henri IV which prepared students for Parisian universities. In the 1920s and 1930s Alain exercised great influence; his teaching was considered exemplary, his books had far-reaching effect. After the First World War he was a philosophical star comparable to Sartre after the Second World War.

Alain's impact was due to his ideas, and also to his personality and his method of philosophizing. He used the induction method, starting with the concrete, the manifest, the banal. From there he moved to the universal. The thinkers towards whom he was oriented were primarily Plato, Descartes, and Kant. His teaching was free, spontaneous, and never dominated by abstraction.

What assured him preeminent standing was his pacifism. Alain stood, according to family origins, in the democratic tradition. He had been a "Dreyfusard," a defender of the Republic against the military-clerical party. As a teacher in the Breton harbor city of Lorient he organized the workers against a possible reactionary insurrection.

Although opposed to war, the 46-year-old registered voluntarily for the army in 1914. He believed that only active participation in the war would give him the right to judge it. His stand earned him a hearing in 1921 when he published his reflections on the war and settled accounts with the "pompous asses," the "cowardly thinkers," and "trained dogs," who glorified the past carnage. Alain believed that, "there are two wars: the one we make and the one we tell about. They have almost nothing in common." He also announced, "speeches are weak and have an impact on the lowest level."[23] He wrote, "we must reduce all power, if we want to have peace."

But Alain did not reject the idea of personally addressing the general public. Starting in 1903, he published short articles, the "Libres Propos," in *Dépêche de Rouen*. These were about all possible questions, both commonplace and eternal, about the pier at Dieppe, about the storm and the elms, but also about Darwin, Dante, Virgil, Victor Hugo, the economic revolution and the "passions." This was philosophizing from the concrete, not for colleagues in the discipline, but for lay people, to help their thinking. Alain carried philosophy into the marketplace like Socrates and the Enlighteners of the French Revolution to whom he declared his allegiance.

His effect was facilitated by his lively and gripping style, clear and aphoristic, a type of dialogue without academic vanity and phoniness. His diction corresponded to that of the people without pandering to vulgar public taste, and he addressed philosophical concerns derived from the Enlightenment. Politically, Alain was a "radical," from the democratic bourgeois party of the same name which exercised a substantial influence in the Third Republic. About his development he reports, "I was born a radical, my father was too, as was my maternal grandfather. This was not true simply because of their views, but rather (as a Socialist would say) because of their class, because they were petty-bourgeois and quite poor. I have always harbored a very strong feeling against tyrants and an egalitarian passion...the instinct was rooted in me."[24]

Proceeding from the concrete, his philosophizing was able to begin at the inkwell and, from there, ascend gradually to the summit. The novelist Andre Maurois, his former student, depicts Alain as a thinker who "tackles a problem directly, as though it were completely new."[25] That is where the first beginnings of an existentialist are to be found, as when he wrote: "To exist signifies a lot; it overwhelms all rational arguments."[26]

Alain rejected all rigid systems that had ready answers for everything, set aside doubt that paralyzed real thinking: "He who plants a small flag on the summit of his thought, as if to say, 'Now I have nothing more to learn,' is ridiculous."[27] Alain also believed, "Thinking is an adventure. No one knows where he will land; if he does, it is no longer thinking."[28]

What Alain taught was less a new philosophy—he proceeded from the old Classicists—than a new type of philosophizing. He did not limit himself to repeating classical theses, but rather went to these sources in order to rediscover the freshness of their genius. What he taught was pre-eminence of mind over matter: "The duty to oneself consists of being free; that means removing the mind from the control of the body and subjecting the body to the spirit...All qualities and capabilities which are not oriented to conscious thought are blameworthy, even if they arise from human kindness."[29]

He was closely associated with the Stoics whom he counted as among the "best teachers." But Alain advocated action, not detachment from the world. Thought is the primary strength, based on the will, which has action as its object: "The will consists of action." Yet this ought not to preclude uncertainty—there was no valid action without critical consciousness: "Uncertainty is the salt of the mind; without a pinch of salt, all knowledge spoils quickly...In fact, one can never believe, one must always test. Disbelief has not yet revealed all that it is capable of achieving."[30] He expressed his sentiment in this succinct statement: "The principle of true courage is uncertainty."

Those of the Enlightenment trusted progress, though not without skepticism. While encouraging action, at the same time they warned of its dangers: "The action always distorts the idea more than is necessary, more than one can suspect. The power of coercion immediately offsets the role of conviction. The mind cannot compel action."[31]

Alain was an opponent of the church though not of the belief in God. In that, he was also a successor to Voltaire and Rousseau. His criticism could be very sharp: "We are poisoned by religion." In 1931 he wrote: "The essence of religion consists in being neither rational nor credible; it is an imaginary cure for imaginary sufferings...Fatalism is the poison in all of these sublime religions in which the human being is no longer anything at all—religions which do not prevent a horrible fanaticism."[32] But Alain also wrote: "It is the sole task of thought to give religion sense," a sense, which the church does not convey, because "the priests are bankrupt." He pointed out the "grave-digger pathos" of the clerics: "One must preach about life, not about death; spread hope, not fear, and promote collective joy, the true human treasure."[33] In this design, religion and art merged into one concept: "Art and religion are not two different things, rather, they are front and back of the same subject."

His suspicion was targeted at every authority: "One must resist all power, that is the most effective and, as one has said, the most provocative attitude toward power. The paths to freedom are still not well known."[34] This passion for freedom approached the anarchistic prerequisite, as did his defense of the individual. Anarchistic inspiration is evident in his statement: "Humanity is always found in the individual; in society, always barbarism."[35] But Alain rejected violent overthrow for fear of "new rulers who will resemble the old ones perfectly." Those socialists who gave priority to society and the state were strangers to him, such a view appeared "barbaric."

The weakness of these tenets was the prevailing ideological tendency to assume the opposition of the individual to society. Moreover, an empirical analysis of the societal scheme was missing completely. Alain rejected the sociology of his time which was formed under the influence of Emile Durkheim. This led his opponents to include him among those who wanted to put an end to individualism. This is a very all-inclusive judgement, its proponents would have had a better understanding if they had had a more thorough grounding in modern sociology.

The heritage of the classical philosophers stood in the way of the progress of his knowledge. Alain's gifted student, Simone Weil, also exhibited these deficiencies; they are regrettably noticeable in her work. Just as categorical was Alain's rejection of psycho-analysis. This is hardly justified since Alain's psychological insights advanced Freud's findings, as when he wrote: "It is the body, not the reason, which causes us to believe." Proceeding from Plato, Simone Weil emphasized a strict dualism between the body and the mind, dismissing Freud's "ambivalence of inner impulses," mental-physiological links and contradictory urges.

To be accepted into Alain's class at the Lycée Henri IV was a distinction. His pupils were a blood brotherhood, loyal to their master. His orientation, which was disposed toward action, was especially attractive to the young. Simone Weil became his best pupil and the most active messenger of his ideas. She owes a lot to her teacher's doctrine—sharply critical analyses, the essential opposition between the individual and society, the prioritization of the intellect, the rejection of authoritarian powers.

Although teacher and student were initially in basic accord, divergences soon made themselves apparent. Simone Weil lacked Alain's skepticism. She allowed his warning about the treacheries of action to go unheeded, always throwing herself into the fight with great zeal. If Alain remained standing carefully on the border of anarchy, then his pupil crossed it at top speed.

As we have already seen, their first contact was cool. To the teacher, the sixteen-year-old appeared a little other-worldly, he called her a "martian" and spoke of her "type-writer-style."[36] Yet the climate soon improved. The teacher's judgement of her: "Excellent pupil who learns, improves and develops with admirable speed and confidence. Her style lags a bit behind her conception, but one can foresee glowing results which will astonish."[37] That settled that—the teacher valued his pupil very highly.

The collected edition of Simone Weil's writings, now in progress, reveals her earliest philosophical thoughts and spiritual beginnings for the first time. The instruction was thorough: at the center, Plato, Descartes, Kant and Alain's admired teacher, Jules Lagneau. In addition, Husserl and Freud, Goethe, Stendhal and Vigny. The author of *Propos* valued the significant literary figures no less than the great philosophers.

Simone Weil began her first philosophical reflection fully in the spirit of Alain: "I am a free being because I am a think-ing creature. A thinking creature alone can be free; that which is not free is the object of thought." She believed that man endows the world with sense. Some passages about the "mind, which effects its future freedom through its present freedom" seem to anticipate Sartre's theses. The same applies to the priority which is accorded to action. "For me, to exist means to act," writes the eighteen-year-old. She will adhere to that; her entire life attest to it.

Existence is thought of in the Platonic sense. By means of its interpretations, thought "creates" existence. "All relations form part of the free mind in so far as it brings about existence." Existence in itself would be senseless; thought alone endows it with value: "Since existence possesses no value, all occurrences, whatever they might be, are useless to him who cannot overcome them. They are only instructive for him who can overcome them." Only action, directed by the mind, endows life with sense.

Yet the pupil exceeds the teacher's doctrine by not limiting herself to the individual: "A single human being can never be free, only humanity can be free." She also includes the idea of action, but not as an individual matter: "One must not search for freedom in solitary actions, but rather in actions which a human being undertakes together with others and for others or with God or for God: for God is the myth of humanity."[38] God is equated with freedom: "To the same extent that I am free, I identify myself with God." Man approaches God by means of his free action: "God is my freedom, He exists in so far as my freedom proclaims itself in my ideas and actions; that is, in so far as I think."[39] The pupil had already expressed religious sentiments—long before her later conversion. Even her remarks about the presence of Christ in Communion were sympathetic, as when she conceded that during Communion "the reason of the faithful is reduced to silence."

Her religious conception at that time corresponded to the pantheism of Alain who equated the figurative God in this world with human striving for justice. This conception distinguishes itself completely from the later, Christian-inspired interpretation. God was identical with the concept of beauty, for beauty would be the "image of God." The same idea is present in all phases of Weil's thought which always links religion with aesthetic criteria, with beauty in literature, music, painting. The pupil appropriated the literary

preference of her teacher—thus her admiration for Stendhal
to whom, in 1926, she devoted her dissertation.[40] There she
states that Stendhal is "an heir to Montaigne, Descartes and
Voltaire." He describes the individual who acts in the midst of
others, yet is as lonely "as in a desert."

This probably expressed the author's feelings toward life:
among other people she always felt lonely. Moreover, she felt
misunderstood by others. Stendhal exhibits a "particularly
French spirit, that of prose," distinct from the poetry of
Shakespeare and Goethe: "This prosaic, Cartesian spirit is
also quite revolutionary and it is no coincidence that, a few
years ago, the country of prose was designated the country
of the greatest revolution. Thus Stendhal ranked with the
authors of the Library of the Citoyen. One could call *The Red
and the Black* the Bible of free people which contradicts the
actual Bible in everything."

This revolutionary declaration is in no way surprising, it
belonged to the Enlightenment philosophy taught by Alain.
More surprising is the passion which is exerted in defense of
Stendhal's hero, the cynical adventurer Julien Sorel: "Julien
acts without any regret; that he has killed does not plunge
him into despair. Only one flaw would he not forgive himself—having no courage." Even in prison he believed he was
"always free in God's view." What enraptures Simone Weil is
the illustration of freedom. To Stendhal, "to the unbeliever,
par excellence" she gives credit for portraying characters
without directing them. He thereby proves himself to be a
real Cartesian: "Stendhal believes in nothing; it is then in the
freedom of the individual which he believes."

The privileging of personal freedom—as we know it—
forms the substance of Simone Weil and Alain's thought.
Indeed, the support for Sorelian-cynicism, which recognizes
nothing but itself and holds all moral norms in contempt, possesses a unique value. However, such a view is not encountered in Weil's philosophy ever again. In this instance, one is

tempted to see the intellectual speculation of a student, her daring interpretation of one of Alain's reflections. There is nothing like this in her later work which refers specifically to the significance of ethical principles, strictly condemning every form of moralism. Noteworthy in the earlier phase is the link with the Enlightenment, as Alain taught her, a link which was effaced after her religious conversion in 1938.

Like her teacher, Simone Weil made use of the short, precise form and a clear style which openly declared its intention. She wrote numerous essays, even a few longer papers, but no systematic, completed work. Fragments predominate by far. The teacher admired his favorite pupil; he characterized her as "surpassing most of her contemporaries, far surpassing." He continued to see her in that way even after their paths separated and Alain had begun to disapprove of the later development of his model pupil. "He combined his praise with a reference to affinities for her way of thinking, he was reminded of himself when he read one of her late political works."[41] Alain himself noted about Simone Weil: "I found her superior to her peers, extraordinarily superior. I have read her commentaries on Spinoza, which eclipsed everything. When she went into politics...I expected a lot." Her first contributions appeared in Alain's publication, *Libres Propos*.

Yet soon she did not limit herself to publishing. She began to be active in the trade union movement, quickly radicalizing the theses of her teacher whose passion was always held in check by his philosophical skepticism. This was not true of the pupil. She felt compelled to translate theory directly into practice: the word into the deed.

3

WITH THE ANARCHIST-SYNDICALISTS

In the Autumn of 1928, Simone Weil began her studies at the Ecole Normale Supérieure which prepared teachers for higher instruction. She also attended some of Alain's lectures and became involved in a variety of other activities, she worked with the trade unions and taught worker education courses. She became a member of the League for Human Rights which was founded during the defense movement for Captain Dreyfus, there she promptly opposed the current course of action which appeared much too moderate to her.

Her revolutionary views were soon known at the Ecole Normale and the director, Célestin Bougle, gave her the nickname, "the red virgin." It was not long before she was approaching Anarchist-Syndicalism. Rejecting Marxist-Leninist doctrine, she considered the authoritarian Communistic Party leadership destructive. Simone Weil did not think about the masses, but rather about individuals. She did not want to lead the workers, but rather, help them lead themselves based on their own needs. Her resistance to an autocratic elite was spontaneous and instinctive, occurring before her consciousness could formulate a theoretical program about it. For Simone Weil, this attitude is pervasive and will persist, despite alterations, until the end. Encouraged by Alain, she discovered the early period of French socialism from the nineteenth century, the Utopians, Proudhon, and Anarchist-Syndicalism before the First World War. She tied herself to this heritage and, although it was discredited, believed it should be rediscovered.

The revolutionary Syndicalists, shaped by Proudhon and George Sorel, had exercised an enduring influence within the French trade unions until 1914. Mostly skilled workers, they had a strong sense of self-confidence and a considerable educational level. Rejecting parties and parliament, they sought to mobilize the worker-masses by means of "direct action." They did not separate their economic goals from moral aims. In contrast to the Marxists, they did not wish for a society of unlimited material benefits but rather for a system for satisfying needs more modest in their nature, yet impacting on everyone. Their ideals were of an ascetic sort. Sorel characterized the class struggle as "social war" and propagated the self-sacrifice of "soldierly virtues." He compared the unions to strict convent orders.

This was extremely attractive to Simone Weil. But this admiration was based on a lot of idealizations. Anarchist-Syndicalism corresponded to an economic structure which was rapidly disappearing. Around the turn of the century in France, craftsmen and small businesses still predominated. Numerically strong, the skilled workers influenced the unions with their individual work ethic. The spread of large-scale industry changed this—now the mass of unskilled workers tipped the scale. The spirit of obedience, acquired in the businesses, also penetrated the worker organizations which could be easily steered by authoritarian leadership cadres. Before the First World War, the anarchistic influence was already diminishing in favor of reforming tendencies. The revolutionaries were not successful in intensifying their strikes. On the contrary, these became steadily weaker and came to a complete standstill around 1910.

After the war, the Anarchist-Syndicalists were still only a small group with a glorious past and a troublesome present. After a brief period of co-operation with the Communist International, they became independent once again. Their influence decreased noticeably as advances were made by the reformers as well as by the Communists. Ever smaller groups of skilled workers, technicians and teachers remained to defend the old tradition. Their voice was the journal, *La Révolution Prolétarienne.* Its contents reflected a superior theoretical level, numbering among its contributors the young Simone Weil.

In July of 1931 she had passed the State examination of *Agrégation* and, in Autumn, assumed her first position, philosophy teacher in a girls' secondary school at Le Puy in central France. There she took an active socio-political role in the teachers' union. She played an even larger role with the mine workers in nearby Saint-Etienne where she became friends with the married teachers, Albertine and Urbain Thévenon. They were traditional Anarchist-Syndicalists and had collected a group of like-minded people around them. Active in worker education courses, Simone Weil dedicated herself, in particular, to the unemployed. She took part in their demonstrations—to the distress of the school authorities who found such behavior unseemly. Finally, she supported the unification of the unions which were split in socialistic and communistic directions. "Working its way into every Trade Union Congress, the split has banished the critical spirit and freedom of expression," she said. "From this, results the complete weakness of the worker class, not damned to poverty alone, but partially robbed of their own function as the base of production—a function which constitutes their dignity."[42]

Despite these calamities, the union remained the basis of Simone Weil's ideology. She believed that the union, not the party, generated the actual proletarian power; this was a consequence of the role of the workers in the production process. "A miner for example, is a revolutionary element in society, not due to his wish to end the exploitation of human beings by other human beings, but by virtue of his role as producer in the mine. This is true because his position as slave vis-à-vis the profit-seeking parasites does not correspond to his real function in production."[43]

This purely economic consideration consciously excluded all other factors such as the intellectual and spiritual. Also ignored were the numerically dominant groups such as middle management, technicians and farmers. This concept was an extreme reduction of Alain's differentiated doctrine. The pupil followed her own path with a materialistic concept which might refer to the opening sentence of *The Communist Manifesto*: "The history of all preceding society is the history of class conflicts." The economy alone is the driving force of history; classes are determined in an exclusively economic way. Therefore, the trade union serves specifically as an organization of workers. Politics was simply rejected; it was nothing more than a "facade," the parties operated in a "vacuum," a ghostly appearance which concealed "real history."

"Underneath politics, real history develops, determined through the action of groups which effect the functioning of the existing societal order. Only through the presence of these groups, thanks to which it functions, can the societal order change at a particular point in time." What was rejected as illusory was real history. The parties were misjudged by the disparaging appraisal that they only provided each other with "phantom struggles." At variance with experience was her insistence that, "the parties cannot influence the real condition of society."

Having amputated the political-intellectual aspect, history presents itself as a skeleton composed merely of economic conflicts of interest. For their defense, the workers require a single organization—the trade unions. But the existing trade unions are not equal to the tasks ahead, therefore new ones must be created. "There are many types of trade unions, but none that consider the present conditions of the worker class," she said. "The trade unions appear as groups which are based not on an analogy to societal functions, but rather on similarity of opinions."

This support of the trade unions and of economic action was based on the model of Revolutionary Syndicalism developed before the First World War. Géraldi Leroy, the editor of these texts by Simone Weil, notes: "The influence of *Reflexions sur la Violence* by Georges Sorel is clearly discernible here."

Evidently, historical experience which made plain the failure of Syndicalism eluded the passionately arguing authoress. The Anarchist-Syndicalist movement was always composed of a minority of the working class and even within the trade union movement they had forfeited their leadership role in the last years before the First World War.

They failed because they showed no understanding of the complicated structure of society. They believed it possible to solve all conflicts with the help of a concise, manichaean formula. Simone Weil idealized this stream of thought to a considerable extent and dispensed with objective analyses. It went unnoticed that Syndicalism was not the unadulterated expression of the working class and that its spokesmen sprang from the intelligentsia, like the journalist Fernand Pelloutier, the engineer Georges Sorel, the lawyer Hubert Lagardelle and the teacher Pierre Monatte. As workers in French society occupied a minority position, the trade unionists, who restricted themselves to the working class, remained isolated. In 1914 only 32 percent of the population was employed in industry, as opposed to 43 percent in agriculture. Fixated on the working class, radical union action was kept from the parliamentary sphere, where the most important decisions were made, by its anti-political align-ment. During the struggles of the Democratic leftists—for the rehabilitation of Captain Dreyfus, for the separation of Church and State—the Syndicalists were not involved because they did not want to bring about the reform of the Republic, but rather its overthrow. This led occasionally to an alliance with the reactionary enemies of democracy and, later, to a complicity with fascism as in the case of Sorel and Largardelle, who became a minister to Pétain. Certainly Syndicalism did not only have negative aspects, but it was not sensible to ignore these aspects as Simone Weil later did, according to her role model, Albert Camus.

In view of the economic crisis, Simone Weil pleaded for a class struggle and against compromises with the capitalists. This stance resembled the Communist course of action at that time which was being pursued under the slogan, "class against class." Here Simone Weil substituted the trade union for the party. She wrote:

> If one does not want to endure the endless alteration between essentially exhausting work in the hope of attaining prosperity and total poverty, then one must declare that there can be no common interest between the exploited and the exploiters. In this case, one must in no way attempt to ease the crisis which could only be accomplished with the approval and under the predominance of the ruling class. Nothing else remains to do than to organize the battle immediately. At the present level of decay, the regime can only survive so long, just as the lack of unity and organization and the want of clear ideas keep the worker class in its current condition of weakness.[44]

Deeds must correspond to words. Simone Weil's out-standing characteristic is this organic unity of thought and action. She sought a practical manner in which to overcome the separation of intellectual and physical labor attained the-oretically by Marx. She did this by meeting with the workers as often as possible, exchanging ideas, allying herself in common action with them, forgoing part of her income in order to live like the poor and finally becoming a factory worker herself.

When, in September, 1931, she began to teach philosophy at the girls' school in Le Puy, her diet was extremely restricted. At midday she went to a modest restaurant, evenings she ate potatoes and drank cocoa, of course without milk. In mountainous Le Puy with its harsh winter, her room remained unheated. She was motivated by her determination to share the life of the poor. Her money for the month lay on the table, available to the needy. In the apartment there was chaos, her books and texts in disarray. Simone Weil did not seek well-being, but rather suffering—this was the source of her happiness. On her weekly trips to Saint-Etienne (six hours round-trip) she carried heavy packs of books for her courses. She found this easy, according to her astonished mother, who made frequent visits in order to try to make her daughter's life more comfortable. These visits in no way pleased Simone Weil.

Here we can see a masochistic tendency which perceived joy in suffering, because suffering expressed identification with the poor and endowed her life with meaning. This quest for suffering, just as much as a quest for happiness, will increasingly determine her thoughts and actions. In her relations with the workers she saw herself as a "leader" by virtue of her knowledge, but she believed that relationships should be characterized by equality.

She began her worker education course by stating: "This is not the start of a series of lectures, but rather an undertaking of mutual instruction. Those who believe they know the least perhaps at the end will be those from whom the others have learned the most. Those possessing the most education should simply be available to the others. You, above all, will determine the form of these gatherings." [45] In Le Puy, Simone Weil was particularly devoted to the unem-

ployed who received hardly any subsidy and lived in extreme
want. She organized a protest movement and forced compromises from the city government. She wrote in the Saint-
Etienne *Tribune Républicaine* on January 9, 1932:

> Those hoping for the end of the unemployment movement
> have deceived themselves. This movement continues with
> increased strength, not, as some people believe it wants to do,
> on a violent path, but rather by means of direct action. Thus
> new compromises were forced...The unemployed must main-
> tain their previous resoluteness and monitor the implemen-
> tation of the hard-won promises. They must force the city
> government to take measures for the benefit of women, the
> elderly and children—measures, which are not limited to a
> mere proclamation.[46]

That the assistant mistress of a girls school behaved so
unusually was a scandal in the petit-bourgeois province. The
press became involved; it was even reported in Parisian
newspapers. A paper in Lyon spoke of a "Moscow activist,"
who undertakes to poison "young girls of the French race"
with pernicious theories. Anti-semitic slogans were useful in
defending the threatened "order." When rebellious Simone
Weil carried the red flag in December, 1933 at the head of a
miners' demonstration, the indignation knew no bounds. She
had already been transferred twice for disciplinary reasons,
now additional disciplinary measures were threatened. The
governing body of the Socialist Party became involved with
the case since it concerned the free expression of its offi-
cials. The agitator received another reprimand.

In March, 1932 she was allowed to inspect a mine, thanks
to the intercession of friends. The very strong impression
made by this experience has been described in numerous
texts. Below ground she took up a pneumatic hammer which
had to be taken away from her, as she was on the point of
working herself to exhaustion with it. She informed her par-

ents: "The visit turned out well. I was allowed to take a pneumatic hammer in my hand. Infernal job..." Her application for employment in the mine was rejected as women were not permitted to work below ground. In the Lyon trade union paper *L'Effort,* she described a "world removed" from all others: "Here in this underground world the people exist only in their capacity as workers; they encounter only fellow workers and the work itself. Everything that surrounds them signifies toil or danger. They view nothing but their tragic fate."[47]

Modern technology made the job of the miner worse. Earlier the tool was adapted to the human body; now the body is controlled by the technical equipment: "The current drama no longer plays itself out between the coal and the human being, but rather between the coal and the compressed air...This machine, adapted not to human nature, but rather to the nature of coal and pressed air, follows in its movements a rhythm foreign to the motions of living which violently subdues the human body." Therefore, it does not suffice to expropriate the mines: a "technical revolution" must put the workers in a position to determine their working conditions. This tenet, confirmed by later experiments with factory work, forms the basis of Weil's criticism of Marx: it would be insufficient to change the conditions of ownership—the working conditions would have to be reformed.

Anti-militarism is a central issue in her work. "Workers have no fatherland." This motto of the *Communist Manifesto* is the guiding principle of Simone Weil's action. The assistant schoolmistress refused to honor the founders of the secular educational system in France, Paul Bert and Jules Ferry, because such a lesson taught patriotism: "The aim was not to liberate the spirit, but rather to replace the church religion with a state religion. That means with a revanchist patriotism, which has recently killed an entire generation of young men." It would now be necessary to defend the secular against the bearers of such an ideology.[48]

When Aristide Briand, France's long-standing Foreign Minister, died in 1932, Simone Weil published a sharp criticism in Alain's *Libres Propos*, in which she characterized the deceased as a war strategist, not a pacifist politician. Briand, she reported, strongly supported the European federation, yet it was only a cover for hegemonic national aspirations.

> He not only represented such politics, he concealed them from view. He viewed these obviously realistic politics as idealistic...He excluded the desire for peace, which had been spreading since 1918, as incompatible with the new form of nationalism and militarism...He had a burial, just as he deserved. Church, army, State were present naturally. Not even the Socialists could be absent.[49]

Simone Weil sarcastically preached a sharp course of all or nothing; gradual reforms were rejected with contempt. Briand, who was attacked fiercely by the militarists and who propagated reconciliation with Germany, was considered as pernicious as the sharpest militarist. The authoress refused to perceive any differences at all.

In the same edition of *Libres Propos*, Alain published a glorification of Briand. He found the text of his former pupil "a little ridiculous." They had gone their separate ways.

Reacting intensely, in her usual way, Simone Weil called Alain's account "truly deplorable."[50] In response to the danger of war she saw no suitable reaction other than the proletarian revolution. All distinction between advocates of an aggressive foreign and military policy and advocates of a defensive policy were ignored. Beyond the revolution there was no salvation. Simone Weil adhered to this position, reminiscent of Lenin's "revolutionary defeatism," for many years. Even in the face of Hitler-German aggression, she did not want to abandon it. She did not consider a European federation a way out at all because Europe had become secondary. "Three new colossi, America, Asia and Soviet-Russia, threaten

Europe's existence," she said. While "the enmity between France and Germany" is "a mere relic of a past epoch."

These are dismaying judgements, whose errors history would soon illuminate. All too impetuously, abstract theories were constructed in place of reality. Indeed, Europe was still far from disappearing from the scene. Internal continental conflicts gave rise to the Second World War, as in 1914 they had led to the First World War. Simone Weil absolutely failed to recognize the true situation: the approach of a new war, with Europe on the center stage.

CHAPTER

4

ANALYSES OF GERMANY

By virtue of the National-Socialists' election success in September, 1931, Germany moved into the international spotlight. Would Hitler seize power and destroy the Weimar Republic? Or would a resistance develop at the eleventh hour and thereby open up a new alternative? The European left, banned from the core of the German workers' movement, vacillated between fear and hope. The radical wing still considered a sudden revolutionary upswing possible. Of course one understood that the German events would be significant for the fate of Europe.

In the circles to which Simone Weil belonged, the interest in German events was keen, the discussion, animated. Events were discussed and analyzed theoretically. The young philosopher took part in these discussions, but that was not sufficient for her. In keeping with her personality, she used her summer vacation in 1932 to travel to Germany. She did not want to observe from a distance, but to be as near as possible to the actual occurrences, informing herself, not being informed second hand. Whenever and however it happened, true to her habit, she wanted to participate directly in the events.

Simone Weil felt herself personally affected by the events in Germany not separated from the Germans by any national barrier. Her impressions appeared in many publications, *La Révolution Prolétarienne, Libres Apropo,* above all in the newspaper of the teachers' union, *L'Ecole Emancipée.* She graphically described the imminent decision, the wait for the announcement of the climax of the drama. "Germany in Expectancy," was Simone Weil's observation. What would occur was expected to be something completely different from events in France. In Germany all questions led to the political sphere: "The questions of human society are posed...every problem, even one about the most intimate aspect of an individual's life, can only be formulated from the viewpoint of societal structure."[51] Indications of a revolutionary situation were accumulating. Meanwhile, passivity, not activity, was conspicuous: "In a constellation, which seems to correspond to the definition of a revolutionary state of affairs, everything is passive."

Her analysis of the opposing parties, which follows, is astonishingly insightful and knowledgeable for a visitor who only spent a short time in the country. The NSDAP (National Socialists), the SPD (Socialists) and KPD (Communists) appear as the main forces: three parties—70 percent of the electorate—which would declare themselves for socialism, though clearly in very different forms. National-Socialists and Communists alone are revolutionary, while Social Democrats and trade unions are characterized as bearers of conservatism. The NSDAP is a disparate movement, consisting of bourgeois, workers, nationalists and socialists, of conservatives and revolutionaries co-operating with big business, as well as divided from it. There is also switching to other parties: the Strasser wing tends toward co-operation with the unions and "strong analogies between the NSDAP and KPD" are unmistakable.[52] Nationalistic, occasionally also anti-semitic, slogans draw the extreme right and the extreme left to each other. "Fiendish perversity" prevents the Communist Party, which rejects a united front with the Social Democrats, from a real breakthrough.

The overall situation was portrayed from a revolutionary perspective. Thus the NSDAP appeared more as a social-revolutionary movement than as a nationalistic one which failed to recognize its most important motivation. Insightful, however, was her reference to the separation of the working class into employed and unemployed, so that there is no unified proletarian class in the Marxist sense. This produces a profound weakness.

This was a sound thesis which made it appear truly daring to speak of a revolutionary situation. Its author herself found: "The crisis has no other effect than to evoke revolutionary feelings in order to continually roll back new sections of the population like waves."[53]

Her analyses were influenced strongly by Trotsky's writings which she knew and regarded highly. Yet on one important point they differed. Notwithstanding his criticism of the KPD, Trotsky considered it a revolutionary party whose errors could be corrected. The strategic aim however, would consist of prevailing over the SPD as a reforming organization. Simone Weil, the French observer, did not share this stance. She felt that, in view of its destructive course, the KPD was just as flawed as the SPD. Not revolutionary phrases but practical, effective actions would be decisive: "The revolution is not a religion in which a bad believer is better than a nonbeliever. It has a practical purpose. With mere words one can no sooner be a revolutionary than a mason or a blacksmith. The only revolutionary action is an action which prepares for a change in the regime or even an analysis and solution which does not simply preach, but prepares for such an action."[54] Requirements of this type were not met by the KPD. On this, Simone Weil based her criticism. She also parted from Trotsky in that she did not consider the Soviet Union to be a

worker-state. Russia represents, she wrote, "various interests of the world proletariat," while the Communist
International is "organically subordinate to those interests."
The posited outlook was gloomy. She depicted a revolutionary situation without hope and doomed to defeat. According
to Simone Weil's impression, the German workers did not
want to capitulate, "yet they are incapable of fighting." This
prediction hit upon the truth exactly. Only a few contemporaries attained such insight. "No people are as susceptible to
effective propaganda as the German people" she said, a statement which would soon secure her importance.

In Berlin, Simone Weil was a guest of a communist worker
family. The new impressions, the encounters with people,
delighted her. "I am getting enthusiastic about the German
people," she wrote to her parents. "No animosity to foreign-
ers, all the people are very nice, especially the streetcar con-
ductors, I find they like me a lot! One sees very few uniformed
Hitler supporters, and even they conduct themselves qui-
etly." This portrayal was a little too idyllic as there were frequent clashes between rightists and leftists, mainly between
Nazis and Communists.

Simone Weil tried to calm her parents who had traveled
to Hamburg to be near her, to be able to help her in an emer-
gency. Their daughter did not want to know anything about
this. With all of her strength she opposed the presence of her
parents.

To her, the situation was actually too quiet. She would
have been satisfied with violent clashes. Disappointed, she
declared, "the Germans are too disciplined for a sporadic
fight." Gladly would this visitor have participated in any dangerous action and she was depressed when she did not succeed in this. However, her encounter with the youth awakened
real enthusiasm: "They don't have enough to eat, but many
forego this necessity in the interest of what makes life worth-
while. They find a few pennies for athletic organizations

which, in spite of all adversities, bring happy boys and girls to woods and lakes...They save on food in order to buy books. Some form study circles where the classics of the revolutionary movement are read, where they write and discuss."

This led her finally to state: "In France there is only young and old, but here there is a youth."[56] Stable French society hardly permitted a political regimentation of the youth. It was otherwise in crisis-shaken Germany where clearly the mobilization of the youth best served the Hitler movement.

All of the impressive qualities of these analyses cannot conceal a number of weaknesses. Disturbing is an economically determined formalism which has classes marching against each other, as though it was a question of carefully assembled armies. The weight of ideological and psychological motivations was misjudged, as when she wrote, "the Hitler party is actually under the control of big business and Social-Democrats are under the control of the German state."[57] This rough framework was based on a materialistic cliche which only considered two strengths: the State and capitalism. There was nothing in between, no extensive number of classes, groups and social strata.

In truth, the NDSAP was not identical with capitalism (Simone Weil soon became aware of this,) nor was the SDP identical with the State. The reality was far more complicated; in both cases it was a question of autonomous powers with their own social roots and political ideas. The NDSAP was, above all, a movement of discontented petit-bourgeois who were mobilized by social, nationalistic and racist demands. The base of the SPD was the historic, traditional workers' movement. In the final phase of the Republic, the State opposed the SPD as an enemy and opened the gateways of power to Hitler. Simone Weil paid little regard to collectively ideological phenomena which, given her idealistic philosophy, is quite incomprehensible. She underestimated the aggressive nationalism as well as the anti-semitism of the NDSAP. The important role of the expanding middle-class, who increasingly surpassed the working class, escaped Simone Weil who continued to let herself be guided by the antiquated model for conflict: capitalism versus the proletariat.

These were serious sins of omission which pointed to a deficient knowledge of sociological research. She seemed to know the writings of Rudolf Hilferding, Ernst Lederer, Henrik de Mans and Hans Speier (and about the meaning of the employed and "mass culture") as little as she did the social-psychological studies of Erich Fromm. Only Ferdinand Fried, an author of the concept of the nationalistic Circle of *Action*, was quoted, which indicates the fragmentariness of her information and her inability to fill these evident gaps.

Certainly this was connected with Simone Weil's intellectual education. One notes her detachment from sociology. This arrogant attitude was part of Alain's doctrine and is found in his pupil. Her analyses of Germany reveal her acumen. Even though she disregarded numerous social factors and remained, to a great extent, on the superficial level, her predictions proved correct. This cannot be said about most of her contemporaries.

In Berlin she encountered Trotsky's son, Leo Sedow, who studied there. He handed over a suitcase with secret documents to her so that she could take it with her to Paris. Simone Weil met with her mother, who accepted the dangerous piece of baggage and brought it safely over the border.

The reports on Germany, with their prediction of the probable victory of the National-Socialist movement, met with only minor approval in Paris. Dismay and indignation against this display of "pessimism" and "defeatism" prevailed. The authoress had too strongly assailed trusted hopes and designs, so resistance was quite natural. The externally imposing German workers' movement still had at its disposal a reputation which paralyzed critical thought. In addition, there was the fear that the German events could be decisive for France: that everything would be altered, that the customary would be called into question.

Simone Weil did not allow herself to be intimidated by such thoughts. She found nothing more unbearable than to let her behavior be determined by fear, to sacrifice her spirit to caution. That was as alien to her as respect for false heros. Events confirmed the pessimistic theses of her reports. However, in February, 1933, Simone Weil still considered "spontaneous movements, strikes, street fighting" possible. Nothing of the kind occurred. In this regard, the observer was all too optimistic. On the whole, she had recognized a lot of things astonishingly well, especially in comparison with other contemporary observers. Her interpretations met with very little agreement but it was her habit to defy the storm.

Soon she was using her experience to draft a new theory of society. Again, she combined theory and practice. When those first persecuted by the National-Socialist dictator came to France, she was an indefatigable helper, assisting with money and shelter. Her parents' apartment stood at the disposal of refugees. Jakob Walcher, functionary of the Socialist Workers' Party, the Marxist historian Paul Frélich, the independent Communist Kurt Landau and Trotsky himself found shelter there.

This activity often turned out dramatically, but sometimes it was disappointing. When this type of involvement proved insufficient, Simone Weil proposed a plan (it was rejected as unworkable) to free a German prisoner and have herself imprisoned in his place—a first project for sacrificing herself, although not the last.

CHAPTER

5

CRITIQUE OF MARX

Simone Weil's German experience provided the basis for a sweeping critique of Marxist doctrine. She formulated her views in two long essays. What happened in Germany—the failure of the best organized workers' movement—was no mere episode, nor was it an event of limited, national significance. She believed that what was at issue was an incident of universal proportion which upset previously accepted theories of society, primarily Marxist but, ultimately, all social-revolutionary doctrines. The idea of the workers as a class which was determined to undo the bourgeois system had become questionable.

"This expropriation is effected through the play of the imminent laws of capitalist production itself," Karl Marx had promised in Das *Kapital*. The theses of the *Communist Manifesto*, stated that the bourgeoisie produced "their gravediggers above all...their downfall and the victory of the proletariat are unavoidable."[58] These principles, which had stimulated and even comforted many generations with the certainty of future success, were called into doubt by Simone Weil in light of historical experience.

Her contribution, "Prospects," was published in August, 1933, in the journal, *La Révolution Prolétarienne.* "Are We Heading for a Proletarian Revolution?"[59] appeared under Sophocles' motto: "Thus I set no value on one who, as a mortal, is warmed by empty hopes." With moral courage as the basis for thought, she was unwavering in opposing strongly held concepts still prescribed by the old dogma. Marx and Engels were still recognized in most leftist circles as ground-breaking thinkers whom critics dared approach only with caution.

Simone Weil totally differentiated herself from those respected thinkers. With powerful blows she shattered the porcelain of the sacred dogma. Her opening makes this immediately clear: "The long-heralded moment has dawned as the development of capitalism is halted by insurmountable barriers...And yet in no epoch did so few symptoms herald socialism." Above all, her analysis is devoted to Soviet-Russia. "No workers' state has been created there, rather a bureaucratic authority which, thanks to the concentration of all political and economic means in their hands, possesses a power until this point unknown." This State is also no "transition regime," as Trotsky asserted. "The oppression of the workers is obviously not a stage in socialism." She believed that his error was evident: He believed "there could only be two state forms, the capitalist state and the worker state. The development of the regime created in October, 1917, contradicts this dogma in no uncertain terms." Capitalism's heir is not socialism, but rather total state dictatorship. Fascism provides an analogous proof, because the Hitler movement is not an agent of capitalistic oligarchy. It has erected a system "whose structure corresponds approximately to that of the Russian regime."

In different countries the power of the bureaucracy was being strengthened within business enterprises: technocratic interests sought to control the state, starting with the economy. This was the case in Hitler's Germany, as well as in Mussolini's Italy, or in the circles surrounding Roosevelt in the U.S. "In view of this state of affairs, one must ask oneself if one wants to consider reality without illusions, whether the successor of the capitalist regime will more likely be a new system of oppression instead of a free union of producers."

The authoress does not leave us in doubt about her view: the bureaucracy has the wind in its sails, technicians and administrative specialists lie ahead. In the undertaking there are three different groups: "workers as passive instruments, capitalists whose authority is based on an existent, decaying economic system, and administrators who rely on a technology whose development increasingly elevates their power."

In comparison to the German Reports, Simone Weil reveals here a finer ability to differentiate. The dualistic model of capitalist-proletariat was given up in favor of a three-dimensional design which granted priority to a new power in society, the technical and bureaucratic specialists. With this prognosis for bureaucratic authority, Simone Weil became a pioneer in the theory of totalitarianism which achieved great popularity after the Second World War, a theory whose advocates included, among others, James Burnham, Hannah Arendt and Karl Dietrich Bracher.

Genuine and modern phenomena which contradicted Marxist doctrine doubtlessly were discovered by the adherents of this theory. On the other hand, their findings were generalized all too quickly. There were bureaucratic phenomena in fascistic, communistic and democratic states. They were not consistently of the same type, yet they served similar goals. In a highly-developed industrial system like Germany, the dictatorship of the state came ahead of other business as opposed to underdeveloped Russia and the democratic U.S. where bureaucratic interests manifested themselves in a completely different manner. Simone Weil failed to recognize such differentiations and reduced everything to a simple formula which signaled hopelessness. This assessment indicated the lack of power of the working class to help emancipate themselves. "The most tragic fact of the present epoch consists of the following: the crisis affects the proletariat more severely than the capitalist class so that it appears as if the crisis is not simply of the regime, but rather of the entire society," she said. History is moving unceasingly toward a global disaster. The workers' movement has failed. "Spontaneous struggle has proven itself continually unproductive, and organized action automatically singles out a leadership apparatus which sooner or later becomes repressive."

This analysis has proven valid to this day. The emancipation mission of the working class has not been achieved anywhere; it was a theoretical design by Marx, bolstered with pieces of Hegelian philosophy. The workers operated most successfully in league with the rising bourgeoisie. On their own they forced social reforms but, where they aimed beyond their own domain they were always defeated. The working class never showed itself to be a force for taking over the leadership of society. Thus the defeat in Germany in 1933 truly had an historically universal significance—the lack of power of the workers' movement to achieve its revolutionary goals became apparent. Fully in keeping with Simone Weil, Andre Gorz speaks of the proletariat as a "copy of the capitalists. Thus the ideology of the traditional workers' movement accepts, renews and completes the work begun by the capitalists: the destruction of the autonomous abilities of the proletariat...The demand based on class is changed into a demand of the masses, that is, into a demand for consumption by an atomized, serialized, proletariat mass which desires to *receive* from society, from power, in reality from the state apparatus."[60]

After half a century Simone Weil's analysis has brilliantly withstood the test of history. The strength of workers has diminished steadily since the 1930's. Because of technical development, their number has melted away at a rapid pace and various groups of technicians, managers and organizers moved into the foreground. Simone Weil was one of the first to point to their significance.

She had no illusions about how her work would be received and expected to be accused of "defeatism." Of course this was no reason for her to forgo her views. She even maintained that she was "not really without hope." But this pointed optimism was unconvincing and did not have the effect of calming enraged sentiments as it was probably supposed to do. Certainly, one must consider that these sentiments never frightened the philosopher, on the contrary they spurred her courage.

A feeling of downfall was dominant, which she rephrased purposefully as merely "being clear" and "understandable." The rising totalitarianism obstructed every way out. Simone Weil compared the situation to the visions of social utopianism in the nineteenth century and found the comparison startling. She recognized a number of flaws in the utopian designs, but to her the development of existing societies appeared still worse. She characterized them as complete systems of oppression, they no longer offered any possibility for influence and reform. That was the projection of the negative utopia of George Orwell's *1984*: the end of history in the form of total authority. The probable end of all resistance efforts was predicated. Moreover, she wrote, no contradiction exists between the theoretical task of clarifying the situation and the practical task of the struggle...Yet the relationship between the two had essentially changed. If one was approaching a catastrophe, which the next epoch would surely bring, then action became senseless. As the calamity was unstoppable, at best a hopeless rearguard action could be provided. This corresponded to Simone Weil's ideal of heroic morality which had replaced the aim of transforming society through a moral creed.

There was no shortage of well-founded and unfounded responses to her work. To the former belonged the reproach that Simone Weil had renounced radical trade-unionism. Among the latter was the charge of "hazardous intellectualism" to the detriment of the organization. The text basically had announced that the emperor had no clothes, the workers' movements had failed. This sharp conclusion is indisputable, even when one shows some understanding for the indignation of the traditionalists in view of such disillusionment. On the other hand, the vision of history, which actually saw the historical process at a standstill, was extremely disputable. This projection of the totalitarian society ruled out all attempts at emancipation for the present era; a deadlock concluded all previous history. It would not be long before Simone Weil herself would give up this negation of history. The confrontation with Hitler's ambitions for power in 1939 would bring about the change, giving rise to a differentiation between democratic and totalitarian states. Her comprehensive essay, written in 1934, *Reflections on the Causes of Freedom and Social Oppression*, developed these already formulated ideas.[61] The piece was first published two decades later. It is basically a criticism of the developed industrial system in which the reproach is leveled that the system oppresses people and destroys nature.

Indeed, Marx declared that he wanted to put an end to this system, yet he failed to achieve that goal. Marx set the task—to increase the powers of production, which were increased by capitalism, still more. That required a cult of production which was nothing but an echo of the capitalistic world-view. Hence her scathing thesis: "Marxism is the highest spiritual expression of bourgeois society." And further: "The task of the revolution, according to its essence, consists not in the emancipation of human beings, but rather in increased powers of production." Marxism assumed that it would achieve its goal through a unified process whereby the technical development would benefit human freedom. Simone Weil did not share the notion of the "moral contentment" which resulted from the expectation of future happiness. She doubted that one would approach an "actual state of paradise where, assured of rich production from little effort, the ancient curse of work broken, the bliss of Adam and Eve before their fall will be rediscovered."

In the Soviet Union such a spirit triumphs—and the result is illuminating: "The entire doctrine on which the Marxist revolution rests lacks every scientific quality." It is a mythology of Hegelian origin. Marx translated Hegel's world-spirit into the economy in order to complete a great mission: "An unending striving for the better."

Such a faith is a religion and the author of *Reflections* rejected it. The development of production would not put an end to the burden of work. Even the abolition of private ownership would not prevent "the labor in mines and factories from burdening those subjugated there even more than would slavery." Increased production does not change this; moreover, it causes a still greater opacity, hinders the possibilities for control, promotes waste of raw materials and causes irreparable destruction to nature. Raw materials are at the point of being "depleted relatively quickly...human beings reproduce themselves, but the iron does not...In general, one thing is certain—the higher the technical level, the more the advantages of new discoveries diminish in comparison with the disadvantages."[62]

Thanks to these discerning views, Simone Weil belongs among the pioneers of ecological awareness. Decades before the *Club of Rome*, her warnings draw attention to actual facts. Opposing the cult of production, whether operated by private or state economic systems, she pleaded for technical restraint, limitation, measure, for a "politics of asceticism" corresponding to the analogous formula of Athanasios Moulakis.

Not to be overlooked is the analogy to the theses of the *Dialectic of Enlightenment*, which Horkheimer and Adorno formulated during the Second World War, concerning a refutation of the traditional expectation of revolution. This applies particularly to the description of turning enlightenment into "mass deception," and to the definition of the technical as power. "Technical rationality today is the rationality of power itself...Yet the wholly enlightened earth glows as proof of triumphing disaster."[63]

In Simone Weil's works, the idea is expressed that the human being has only escaped the power of nature to the extent that he has subjected himself to the power of other human beings. "Nature thereby loses its divine quality gradually," she states. "The deity increasingly assumes human form."[64]

Similarly, according to Horkheimer and Adorno, "the way in which human beings manifest a likeness to God consists in their sovereignty over their existence within view of the Lord in command."[65] Decisive here, as above, is the anticipation of an unstoppable, spreading catastrophe, the awareness of leaving behind nothing but a "note in a bottle" for future generations. Certainly, Simone Weil's methodology is more direct, easier to grasp. Her critique of Marxism is undisguised in contrast to the academic style of the philosophers of the Frankfurt School. Their viewpoint on the other hand, contradicted the aesthetic ideal of this French woman. What she sought was not maximum production and satisfaction of desire, but rather the reduction of gigantic organizations to modest means, the humanizing of production, which in return granted greater respect to workers' thoughts.

Simone Weil did not want to reduce labor to a minimum, as Marx aspired to do. She believed that "the dignity of the producers should be established as pre-eminent." Guided by Proudhon, she again followed the ideal of the old skilled worker who, thanks to the earlier machine tools, represented "perhaps the most beautiful type of worker." Simone Weil did not see the ideal in the future, but in the past. She believed that automation and the dehumanizing of labor are consequences of the great emphasis on industry.

"Couldn't an industry divided into numerous small enterprises give rise to a reverse development of machine-tools, and also to more deliberate and sensible forms of labor, than are required by the most skilled work in modern operations?" This question is valid today as, with great urgency, the rapid technical revolution reduces human beings to mere helpers of electronic devices.

Reflections distinguished itself from Marxist doctrine at yet another central point. The economy is not designated as the main force of history, the primary force is instead the political-military power struggle for the defense or conquest of privileges. The political situation possesses a weight of its own and frequently also determines the economic processes. The power struggle culminates in war; war becomes the destiny of mankind—unchanged since the time of Homer.

Later she would write, "the true hero, the true theme, the focus of *The Iliad* is power. This power, which uses people, which subjugates people, in the face of which people tremble."[66] The expanding power of the state moves unceasingly to war: "The axle, around which the thus altered society turns, is nothing other than the preparation for war."[67] Even the construction of communist states could not change that; even they, as the example of the Soviet Union teaches, would be drawn into the power struggle. Criticism was leveled against scientific organizations. Thanks to them, science became an institution of authority. This was also the case in the workers' movement where the intellectuals possessed "the same privileges as in bourgeois society." The suggestion that the different spheres of science be made comprehensible to all was certainly dubious. As nice as this idea might be, in view of the furious expansion and complexity of knowledge, this hope from the early period of humanism had to show itself to be more than illusory.

The essay drew its essential impulses from the substance of anarchistic thought. It invoked the negation of the state, anti-historicalism and the emphasis on individual freedom. "Rejecting the subordination of the individual within the collective, the refusal causes the individual's destiny to be subordinate to the course of history."[68]

This corresponds to the spirit of anarchism; no Marxist could have written it. Yet *Reflections* separates itself from anarchism, which acceded to a hopeful belief in progress, through its essential doubt that it is possible to overcome the existing condition and construct a better society. Cited as mere illusions are "the belief that one can turn the switches of history in another direction through reforms or revolutions with the help of a change in the regime and the hope for a defensive or offensive action against tyranny and militarism. These are daydreams." Nothing exists upon which even simple endeavors could be based. Marx's formula, whose outcome was that the regime would produce its own grave-diggers, is refuted fiercely every day. One questions how Marx was ever able to believe that slavery can give rise to a free people. Never in history has a slave regime collapsed under the blows of the slaves.[69]

Here, too, the unavoidable, at the very least the probable, downfall, comes as the conclusion. The author, impelled to action, had brought herself to an impasse, her thought robbed action of all sense. There was, however, a sentence which suggested another direction: "No help can be expected from the people..." Still cautious, she heralded a turning point which would soon give a new focus to her thought. If people are no longer offered any hope, than hope can only be found in transcendence beyond the visible world.

In spite of her pessimistic pronouncement, she was in no way dejected. Indeed, she boasted of having achieved "a wonderful freedom of conscience." Here one finds a constant—

danger produces no horror, rather it evokes joy. Personal feelings tip the scale and the destiny of others becomes less interesting. The ego takes priority—a characteristic which is very typical of Simone Weil's behavior in contradiction to the evidence of her altruism.

With its lofty, intellectual emphasis, *Reflections About the Causes of Freedom and Social Oppression* constitutes difficult reading. In limited space, many themes are dealt with, sometimes only sketchily. There is the example of manipulation by the media: "With the help of the mass media, the press and radio, one can have an entire people swallow ready-made, and accordingly absurd, opinions at breakfast or supper because even reasonable views become distorted and false when accepted without reflection. In this way, one cannot produce a single flash of intelligence."[70] This is a brilliant perception whose value should be highly respected in view of the current power of television.

The essay seems to have been composed quickly and fluently with few revisions. As always she wrote in a round, even somewhat childish handwriting. Although expecting a catastrophe, she was in no way dismayed. Finally, missing from the text are references to sources that might have influenced Simone Weil. One thinks here, above all, of Georges Sorel, Vilfredo Pareto and Gaetano Mosca with their emphasis on the power struggle and the dominance of the "political class." Perhaps also named would be Max Weber and the historians of *Annales,* Marc Bloch and Fernand Braudel, whose delineations considered a multitude of historical forces—economic, governmental and ideological.

The categorically preaching style endowed the text with the aura of prophecy which is not exactly conducive to a substantive analysis. Next to perceptive insights one encounters dubious simplifications. Questionable is the reduction of general history to a power struggle—a formula happily employed by militant Social-Darwinists—which disregards

numerous other factors. Also questionable is the undifferen-
tiated equation of all states, whether democracies or dicta-
torships. Another dubious point is the exclusive
identification of the state with destruction, while functions of
structure and preservation are ignored. The prediction of a
totalitarian age, as well as that of the hopelessness of all
resistance, proves false.

The conflict between the individual and the collective as
a pre-eminent historical force was also an abstract sketch, in
that personal freedom alone appeared to be in opposition to
society. This failed to recognize human beings as social
organisms, as members of the collective who did not stop
belonging to society even when at a variance with it.

Simone Weil rejected the revolutionary process as a "daydream" but her own theory deserves the same name. She
expressed it thus: "Freedom is only an ideal, in reality as
impossible as drawing a perfectly straight line with a
pencil."[71] It was the projection of an unobtainable ideal. She
also named that which stood in the way of freedom, "the
complexity and scope of the world." Consciously she dispensed with taking into account the complex state of affairs.
More than anything else, her theory had the effect of bring-
ing about personal happiness, "a wonderful freedom of conscience." The reproaches of others had no impact. She saw
Marx's concept of revolution as lacking in "all scientific character," yet this also applied to Simone Weil's own views.
Methodologically the greatest confusion reigned. The author
of *Reflections* made use of scientific criteria in order to identify the weak spots in other theories, yet, in the depiction of
her own concepts, she dispensed with scientific method in
favor of a doctrine of pure personal instinct. The concept of
the individual relieved from every societal constraint is an
illusion. Simone Weil believed that skilled workers of the
early industrial era approached the ideal. This view ignored
reality, for even those qualified workers belonged to an indus-

trial hierarchy which was subject to the mechanisms of power. The skilled workers received directives from superior authorities and issued them to their subordinates. At no time has there been an authority-free state of affairs as conjured up by Simone Weil. This, too, was nothing but a daydream.

Alain did not hide his skepticism. In a letter written in 1935 he said, "I am quite certain that indignation alone would be incapable of alienating you from your calling. Remember what I have told you: that which is misanthropic is wrong." Insightfully, he had revealed the signs which could lead his pupil from a critical to a prophetic standpoint. The teacher had perceived correctly, yet his warning was in vain. Simone Weil turned more and more strongly away from Alain's skeptical doctrine which generally equated doubt with thought: "With his famous doubt, Descartes did nothing except think." Such criticism was not likely to deter this rebellious woman. On the contrary, she drew strength and confidence from her position. What is discernible here is a self-confidence which loves elevating itself above others to demonstrate individuality and uniqueness.

A daring critic, she encountered some praise, although certainly more condemnation. At that time she became friends with Boris Souvarine who, as a dissident Communist, did not share most of her views yet was tolerant and interested enough to take them seriously. Less pleasant was her encounter with Trotsky, who spent the end of December, 1933, at her parents' house across from the Jardin du Luxembourg. The Russian revolutionary, in France since the summer of the same year, was seeking supporters but he did not tolerate contradiction. That the 24-year-old dared to criticize the famous Bolshevik leader disconcerted him. He accused her of "clinging to a legal, logical, and idealistic spirit."[72] To which she responded: "Your adherents are the ones who think idealistically because they view an oppressed class as ruling."

Simone Weil refused to define the Russian workers as the ruling class. Finally, Trotsky asked: "Why do you doubt everything?" The believer had revealed himself to the skeptic. She commented on the discussion as follows: "Basically, Trotsky and Lenin have played a role analogous to that of the great capitalists in the era of 'progressive' capitalism—at the cost of thousands of human lives."

6

PRACTICAL EXPERIENCE

The factional struggles of the left wing radical groups disappointed Simone Weil. The groups' activities were restricted by intellectual narrowness and personal intrigues that were hard for her to bear. Simone Weil's pessimism was confirmed. A few years later she wrote to the novelist Georges Bernanos, "Since childhood my sympathies belonged to those groups who related to the despised classes of the societal hierarchy. But then it occurred to me that the behavior of these groups was inclined to destroy all sympathy."[73]

The ubiquitous dogmatism and the vindictive clashes between cliques were alien to her. She was suspicious of the intellectuals' air of authority as they posited themselves as the workers' leadership elite. Her view of such behavior, formulated in *Reflections*, was based on experience. Simone Weil altered her thesis to take an anti-intellectual position, paired with a turn toward the lower classes, the disenfranchised. This mistrust of the intellectuals was, not lastly, also an expression of hate toward herself—the heavy-weight intellectual.

The decision to work in a factory was a result of her discontent with her life up to that point. She found it intolerable that intellectuals theorized about labor without being

acquainted with it in a practical sense; that they pretended to
lead the workers without knowing who the workers were. The
intellectuals' remoteness from practical experience horrified
her. She was appalled that the great Bolshevik leaders like
Trotsky and Lenin who had vowed to create a free working
class had probably never set foot in a factory. As they "had
not the faintest notion of the actual conditions which determine the serfdom or freedom of workers...politics appear to
me to be a nasty joke."[74] While on vacation from school, the
assistant school-mistress was hired by the Alsthom Electric
Plant as a temporary worker in December, 1934, through Boris
Souvarine's intervention. The conditions were oppressive,
seemingly a kind of hell. In the operations, the employer's
hierarchy was in absolute control. The trade unions were
weak, often represented poorly or not at all. Unemployment
depressed wages and held the workers in check.

Simone Weil was not accustomed to physical labor. She
had a weak constitution, was plagued by headaches and ear-
aches and, moreover, she was clumsy. According to an ironic
self-characterization, she was "hanging around in the working
class." Factory work was drudgery for the assistant school-
mistress, incomparably more so than for the average worker
who was better suited to the factory conditions.

In this respect, her *Factory Journal* describes a personal
experiment more than the general situation of the working
class. Naturally, conditions of common significance are
revealed: outside control, subjection to an authoritarian
order, and a production plan imposed from above. But her
very subjective feelings appear through the prism. Her
impressions were sharper and more painful because a completely new, unknown world was discovered. These were not
the impressions of a laborer who operated under conditions
which had been familiar to her since her childhood. Simone
Weil's experiences were much more those of a bourgeois
woman who is acquainted with comfortable living conditions

and knows that her time in the factory is of short duration. This separates her, of course, from the real proletarian experience. Yet, even given this, it is noteworthy that nowhere but in Zola's depiction of the mine in the novel *Germinal* are the conditions of industrial factory work illuminated and expressed more sharply and more penetratingly.

The young philosopher stamped sheet metal into parts; she did not meet the quotas. She experienced "intense headaches, very slow and miserable...terrible, sore eyes...great fatigue." Consequently, the report of the experiment characterized it as "slavery." The power of superiors' orders was perceived as degradation; there was no appealing their decisions, even in regard to dismissal. Trade unions did not exist, resistance was, at best, mute protest. Simone Weil had to work at an oven which she characterized as "very tiresome work. Unbearable heat, the flames leap up at my hands and arms...on the first evening, around five o'clock, I completely lose control of my movements from the pain of the burns, from exhaustion and headache."[75] Despairing, and yet happy to experience this, she believed she had found some brotherhood in the factory. But this occurred only in rare cases, most easily with the skilled workers whose tasks demanded constant attention, reflection, quiet and a leisurely pace. The situation was otherwise with the temporary workers whose tasks required minimal thought and involved great physical strain. A numbing dullness was the result. In the words of the young philosopher, it was: "the highest level of degradation." In discussions with the laborers, social questions, issues of union or party, were never mentioned. In the canteen the workers read only bourgeois newspapers. Resignation prevailed and even affected Simone Weil:

> The exhaustion allows me to forget the real reasons for my time at the factory and makes the strongest temptation of this life almost insurmountable—to no longer think. This is

the only means to avoid suffering. Only on Saturday after-
noon and on Sunday do memories and fragments of ideas
return. I *even* remember to be a thinking creature. Horror
seizes me as I observe my dependence on external circumstances: it would suffice for them to force me one day to a job
without a weekly day-off—which ultimately is always possible—and I would become a beast of burden, obedient and
submissive (at least in my eyes.)[76]

She continues: "Revolt is impossible." A pre-requisite for
resistance is physical strength; weakness must be overcome,
avoid moral decay or become dull and deadened.
Submissiveness was particularly characteristic of the female
workers. Although unhappy, they were not to be moved to
resistance: "They are not the slightest bit interested in the
machines or production. Resigned, with fits of powerless
revolt, they dream of something better in the way of individual happiness, like winning the lottery, etc."

Ear infections and anemia forced Simone Weil to inter-
rupt her work on January 15th for one month. She found rest
in the Swiss mountains where she stayed with her parents in
a house of friendly German refugees. In April she began work
again, but only for a month. She was unemployed until she
was hired as a machinist at Renault on June 5, 1935. There
she noted: "The production supervisor resembles the King of
France. He delegates less pleasant functions of his authority
to his subordinates; the pleasant ones he reserves for himself."

Her colleagues were friendly: "When one has the chance
to exchange a glance with a fellow-worker—in passing, when
one asks for something or watches him at work—his first
reaction is to smile. Very charming. This is only the case in a
factory."[77] Yet she did not find the great, expected brotherhood, the comprehensive solidarity she sought.

Simone Weil held the unions responsible for the behavior
of the workers, for their "bourgeois mentality" which inhib-

ited their motivation. While they were concentrating primarily on wage demands during the period of prosperity, they had assisted "in degrading and corrupting the worker class."[78] She found Marx's demand for "breaking wage-slavery" sensible, yet trade unions were supposed to concern themselves less with wage questions than with the general working and living conditions of the employed—which she included under the heading of "human dignity."

There were only a few signs of solidarity: "Generally, even the relationships between the workers reflect the harshness which controls everything inside the factory," she wrote to her friend, Albertine Thévenon.[79] Nonetheless, every human gesture in the factory had a much greater value than the polite, empty words in privileged society. These had no weight. In the factory alone, "does one know, what brotherhood means."

This experiment was painful. "This encounter with unhappiness killed my youth," she wrote in retrospect. Yet she was happy to have had the experience. It was, to her, "real life," in contrast to the pretence of her earlier existence. "This experience, which meets my expectations, is, nonetheless, separated from them by an abyss: it is reality, no longer imagination. It was not this or that idea that was changed (many, on the contrary, have been confirmed,) ultimately it was much more, my entire view of things, my actual concept of life."[80]

In a letter addressed to Boris Souvarine, she revealed the motive for her actions. She never felt the need to flee from the factory: "Because I do not perceive this suffering as mine; I perceive it as the suffering of the workers, and whether or not I myself endure it, appears to me to be a rather incidental detail."[81] In a passion, she took the lot of all sufferers upon herself. This is the prominent feature of her character, evident since childhood when she withstood deprivations in order to help the soldiers at the front. In all phases of her later life this impulse will burst forth with increasing persistence and self-confidence. The experiment had shaken her faith in the revolution. On August 22, 1935, she ended her job at Renault, writing to her university friend, Claude Jamet: "The revolution is impossible, because the revolutionary leaders are incompetent. But the revolution is also not desirable because they are traitors. Too stupid to achieve victory, and if they had it, they would crush it exactly as in Russia."[82] These were somewhat superficial judgements though, the young philosopher had already expressed herself more thoroughly on this subject.

At the end of August, before the start of her new position in Bourges, she traveled to Portugal with her parents. There she was influenced by a procession of fishermen's wives—the first approach of Christianity: "The fishermen's wives stepped around the boat during the procession, carrying candles and singing very old songs of heart-rending sadness...There I suddenly experienced the certainty that Christianity is the real slave religion, for slaves who cannot help but belong to it—exactly like myself, among others."[83]

Simone Weil's thought process was in an interim phase. In motion, it loosened itself from former principles and was about to explore anew—though nothing as yet had assumed any particular form. Teaching at the girls school in Bourges, she dedicated herself to Greek poetry and Gregorian music and attended early masses at the cathedral.

At the beginning of 1936, there was an exchange of ideas with the manager of the Rosiéres hat factory who edited a plant newspaper. The assistant school-mistress would collaborate on it. Moreover, she hoped to be hired as a laborer in the factory. The paper published her essay about Antigone, which did not exactly correspond to the customary content of a factory paper, and probably demanded too much from the readers. Other projects about Greek culture, about Electra, were not realized. The encounter between the factory manager and the philosopher turned out disappointingly, as both sides had attached different expectations to it.

The planned collaboration was stuck from the beginning. The manager was anxious to improve the social climate in the business without changing the existing conditions. Simone Weil, on the other hand, wanted to address the workers so that she herself could report on their situation. In this way, the workers were supposed to overcome their "feelings of inferiority" and to recover "a sense of their own dignity." The manager rejected the project, which would allow the workers to speak, as an incitement to class struggle. Letters were exchanged between them but the collaboration was at an end.[84] The mild, appeasing intentions of the factory manager were in opposition to Simone Weil's creed:

> Human relations are only thinkable for me on the basis of equality. As soon as someone treats me as a subordinate, in my eyes, a human relationship between him and me is out of the question. I treat him as a superior, that is, I endure his power exactly as I would endure cold and rain...Natural inequalities exist. In my opinion, considered from a moral standpoint, a societal organization is only good to the extent that it strives to reduce inequalities (naturally toward a higher, not a lower level.) It is bad to the extent that it aggravates inequalities. It is, finally, destructive, when it erects insurmountable barriers.

Here stubborn pride revealed itself, a feeling that dignity was the absolute expression of human existence. There was her constant preoccupation with Antigone who fascinated Simone Weil and to whose spirit she felt herself bound. Antigone's rebellion against the king's decree, her personal creed in opposition to governmental power—this was an unequalled role model. Like the Sophoclean heroine, this modern rebel could cry out: "See if you want to dare it, to undertake it." She too heard words like those which the fearful Ismene cried to her sister, Antigone: "You want what never succeeds."

The majority of workers were far from such heroic feelings. In the factory Simone Weil had observed mostly resignation, passivity, even "complete submission." Yet at the same time something important escaped her—processes, which occurred in the sub-conscious of the working class or, beyond the factory, in the political sphere.

The situation in France began to change with the leftist offensive. After the people's front had gained a majority in parliament on May 5, 1936, the new government was under the leadership of the Socialist Leon Blum. Mass strikes broke out and factores were occupied. Two million people took part in the actions. Simone Weil was enthusiastic and communicated her view to the manager of the Rosiéres hat factory: "You will certainly not doubt the feelings of joy and unspeakable release that the strike movement has brought to me. The results will be, what they can be. But they can neither erase the value of these beautiful, happy days of comraderie, nor the relief felt by the workers when they saw that those in power yielded once to them."

The movement, with its surprisingly powerful dynamic, achieved a range of social reforms: a 40 hour week, paid vacations, and the right to participate in unions. Simone Weil's writings, which emphasized above all the resignation of the working class, had anticipated none of this. Her proverbial contempt for the political sphere was responsible for her failure to comprehend the situation. Concentrating on factories and unions alone, the problems of the battle against fascism escaped her, problems which affected the workers more than she understood.

During the mass strikes, she visited the Renault factory in which she herself had worked. After the reunion with her "buddies," she described the prevailing mood: "Completely independent of the demands, this strike is a joy in and of itself, a pure joy, an absolute joy."[85] The employees were united by a powerful feeling of solidarity: "the brotherhood," which she had hoped for for so long. It would not be a lasting success, only a brief moment of glory. Nonetheless, one lesson remained: "Today one can no longer ignore the fact that those whose only role on this earth is supposed to be to bow down and be silent, only bow down and keep silent to the extent that they cannot do otherwise."[86]

This was different from the revolutionary left with its slogan "everything is possible." She declared herself for limited goals of the reforming type. According to her, the working class had obtained rights for which they were not prepared. In order to make use of them, responsibility was necessary: "One only retains one's rights when one knows how to safeguard them properly."

Simone Weil studied the labor conflicts in northern France—an exemplary field analysis[87] in which she warned that the strikes could slip away from the unions and go out of control. The young philosopher maintained solidarity with the unions only up to this point because she did not trust the organizations. Working from this "basis," she sought to strengthen the unions. A change in her thinking stood out clearly. The shop stewards chosen in the businesses were supposed to subordinate themselves to the union. After the overthrow of the old authoritarian order in the factory, the unions were presented with the task of setting up a new order, together with the employers, which would avoid the arbitrariness of the past system. "But industry cannot exist without order." New forms of labor and modes of discipline would be tested. A new way of thinking, constructive measures, declared themselves; meanwhile the Anarchist-Syndicalist utopia began to fade.

On June 18, 1936, the Civil War began in Spain. On August 8th, Simone Weil crossed the border at Portbou in order to support the Republicans' struggle. Her last revolutionary engagement ended not two months later on September 25th. Totally unsuited to being a soldier, her participation was hardly of any use. Initially a member of the famous Durruti's anarchistic militia, she was withdrawn after one week to perform kitchen duty. Because she was very short-sighted, her foot knocked into a cauldron of boiling oil and the injured Simone Weil entered a military hospital. She was ultimately cared for by her parents who hurried there and brought her back to Paris.

She had hurried to Spain in order to be with those who were engaged in the struggle. In addition, she wanted to have the right to vouch for her convictions and, what is more, to sacrifice herself for them. In the draft of a letter to the novelist George Bernanos, Simone Weil had observed that even more than the war, she abhorred those "who holed themselves up in the hinterland." Furthermore, she tried to be entrusted with a perilous mission in the territory controlled by Franco's troops: she wanted to rescue the leader of the marxist POUM, Jacques Maurin, who was hidden there. When this unrealistic suggestion was rejected, she joined the anarchistic militia.

Her *Spanish Journal* is the report of a growing disillusionment.[88] Her first impression was enthusiastic: "Power belongs to the people. The men in blue work suits command. This is one of the rare moments, until now never lasting long, when those who always just obeyed are taking over the leadership." Yet the joy soon disappeared. In the small troop on the Aragonne front, confusion and incompetence ruled; there was no synthesis of authority and freedom. She observed: "Organization is via elected delegates. No special knowledge. No authority. They pay no heed to the qualifications of the military technician." Since the militia took no prisoners, outright massacres were the result. Nonetheless, Simone Weil asserted that she had no fear: "If they apprehend me, they will kill me...But that is well-deserved. Those on our side have spilled enough blood. I am a moral accomplice."

This struggle corresponded in no way to the philosopher's ideal notions. In the draft letter to Georges Bernanos who, although politically to the right, disapproved of the violent deeds of Franco's troops, one finds her taking stock of the Spanish experience.[89]

What filled Simone Weil with the most indignation was the general bloodthirstiness:

> I had the personal feeling that the secular and spiritual institutions isolated a group of human beings from those whose life possesses a value. For the human being, nothing is more natural than to kill. If one knows that it is possible to kill without enduring sin or censure, then one kills...It is a seduction, an intoxication, which is impossible to resist without a true magnanimity, which I must consider to be unusual as I have encountered it nowhere.

She found that formerly peaceable people could share such bloodthirstiness and declared: "I could never feel any respect for those in the future." Later she confessed to Father Perrin that she feared the threat of analogous passions in herself: "Because I felt their possibility in my soul, they terrified me." The unrestrained violence destroyed the meaning of the conflict: "Such an atmosphere immediately obliterates the aim of the struggle. For one can only formulate the aim with regard to the public welfare, to the welfare of human beings—but there human beings are worthless."

The anarchistic organizations were "an astonishing mix," where the bad was combined with the best. The idealists predominated, nonetheless there was "a trench" which separated the anarchistic soldiers from the unarmed peasants: "a trench, which fully resembles the one which separates the poor and the rich...Filled with the spirit of sacrifice, one sets out as a volunteer and one happens into a war which resembles a mercenary war, only with even greater cruelty and even less respect for the enemy." To Georges Bernanos, the monarchist, she asserted: "I feel incomparably closer to you than to my militia comrades in Aragonne—those comrades whom I loved."

The conduct of the Spanish Anarchist-Syndicalists who, above all in Catalogia had influential mass organizations at their disposal, had disappointed her. Some parallels to Lenin's politics are discernible. The old military penal code with the death penalty for insuring discipline was reintroduced. Anarchistic newspapers yielded to a campaign of harassment "which perhaps exceeded that of the French press during the war. What concerns the police is thus acknowledged publicly: in the course of the first three months of civil war, oversight committees, responsible functionaries and irresponsible individuals undertook executions without the pretence of a court and beyond any authority. On the front, sixteen-year-old children are shot if they are captured with a weapon during a battle."[90]

Such observations brought about a complete change of orientation. The end of the social-revolutionary engagement left behind disillusionment and bitterness. The path was clear for a new hope, this time symbolized by religious faith. The experience of the Spanish Civil War strengthened her pacifistic conviction. Simone Weil rejected a war against Hitler and Germany and said she was cured of all "naive patriotism." She stated, "the humiliations, which my country can inflict on other countries, are more painful to me than those which it would have to bear."

7

WAR

In Simone Weil's view of history, war, with its devastating force, forms an axle which drives all events. Based on this, all issues can be understood. Again and again she invoked *The Iliad*, where a fateful war, inflicted by the Gods, was a metaphor for human existence. She called Homer's work a "Poem of Force" in an essay published in *Cahiers du Sud in* 1940-41. According to her, *The Iliad* was the first "wondrous expression" of the Greek spirit, just as the gospel was its last testimonial. The Iliad depicted war without euphemism and without hate. Later she invoked it in order "to cover it with glory...Nothing that the peoples of Europe have created equals that first well-known poem which sprang from one of their own. Perhaps they will rediscover the epic genius in it when they know nothing apart from fate, when they no longer admire force, never hate enemies nor condemn the ill-fated. One has to doubt, whether this will happen soon."[91]

For this philosopher, the most important spiritual source is Greece. From it, she will continuously derive reasons for her admiration. The Hellenic spirit provides her with guidance and is interpreted in a very personal way for very real aims. Simone Weil draws a message of peace from *The Iliad*.

However, in that work, war appears as an unavoidably imposed fate, doubts arise about the feasibility of peace. The significance of war, so she writes, consists of changing human beings into objects, this adapts them, in turn, to slavery: "Thus nature is force. Its power to transform human beings into objects is of a doubled sort and it takes effect in a twofold direction. In a way which is different, yet the same, nature petrifies the souls of those who suffer it as well as those who control it."[92]

She referred to the underestimation of the impact of war in the Marxist conception. In that Marx sought to explain everything with the concept of class struggle, he was guilty of an unacceptable simplification:

> He neglected war as a factor every bit as important to human history as social struggle. Therefore, the Marxists always found themselves in a ridiculous confusion in the face of all the problems posed by war. This omission is significant for the entire nineteenth century. With this approach, Marx gave further proof of how dependent intellectuals were on the controlling influences of the time. At the same time, he wanted to forget that the internal struggles among the oppressed and among the oppressors are just as meaningful as the struggles between the oppressed and the oppressors. Moreover, the same person could be both oppressed and oppressor. Marx situated the concept of oppression at the center of his work without ever analyzing it.[93]

Today such statements are hardly ever challenged. Here a gap in Marxism is indicated and its weakness is revealed especially clearly. Simone Weil's views also fit in with the findings of psychology, which, in contrast to the Marxist interpretation, define the human being as the sum of contradictory impulses. In the Marxist view, the human being appears as uniformly structured, controlled by reason, and motivated by economic interests. This had once also been the viewpoint of the social revolutionary, Simone Weil, yet gradually she moved on to a differentiated, psychological concept which better corresponded to reality.

Her opinion of war was unmistakable. She held that even in the approaching totalitarian society, militarism would be the decisive mainspring. The workers' movement continually displayed confusion in the face of war, vacillating back and forth between militaristic and pacifistic ideas. Marx and Engels were supporters of a "progressive war." Later the Bolsheviks rejected imperialistic war, but only with an eye toward their goal of conducting their own revolutionary war. Proudhon was also a military patriot. According to Simone Weil, "one view was common to all of those theories—the categorical refusal to understand war in and of itself."[94]

In 1933, in keeping with Alain's doctrine, Simone Weil had characterized war as a factor which transformed "power into despotism and slavery into murder."[95] A future military conflict would strengthen the state apparatus, increase its control over the economy, and reduce human values. Her rejection of a war against Hitler's Germany was based on this. Any national campaign, even the call for a boycott of German goods, was repudiated since this would establish a partnership with the bourgeoisie under the rubric of patriotism which would be harmful to the workers. "Nothing can be more dangerous for the proletariat than national passions since these always lead to a type of truce which is useful to the bourgeois state."[96] Simone Weil considered the Treaty of Versailles an injustice and blamed the workers' movement for not having rebelled against it distinctly enough. Consequently, she faced the German problem with a guilty conscience which influenced her entire way of thinking: "For us the only means of combatting Hitler consists in showing the German workers that their French comrades are ready to put forth effort and sacrifice for them."[97]

The axiom invoked again and again was that war represented the highest escalation of the oppression already in effect during peace: "An enduring and almost systematic degradation is an essential factor of our society's organization in peace, as in war; but in war this is true to a far higher degree."[98] This absolute pacifism will be her guiding principle until 1939. One would have to choose between national prestige and peace. She wrote in 1936: "Whether one appeals to the fatherland, democracy or revolution, the politics of prestige always mean war."[99]

Extremely consistent as always, Simone Weil defended her viewpoint to the point of delusion. Thus, she approved of the politics of "non-intervention" of the People's Front government of Léon Blum, which ruled out supplying arms to the Spanish Republic. This action was supposed to ensure international approval under the watchword of neutrality. One could only preserve peace "when the principle of neutrality completely takes the place of the lethal principle of mutual assistance."[100] She knew that with this she condemned the anti-Franco coalition in the Spanish Civil War to defeat because the Republicans "replaced the canons which they lacked with their own flesh." She also knew that, "the freedoms of the French people are closely tied to those of the Spanish people." It was not to be overlooked that this "generalized non-intervention" could result in the gradual suppression of the people through fascism. Nonetheless, Simone Weil clung to her view: "If we were willing to sacrifice the Austrian miners, the starving farmers of Aragonne and Castille, and the anarchistic workers of Barcelona to prevent a world war, then nothing in this world can induce us to foment a war. Nothing, neither Alsace-Lorraine, nor colonies, nor treaties. One should not be able to say to us that something in this world is more precious than the life of the Spanish people."[101] After the sacrifice of Spain, a halt can no longer be called, according to her logic. Unavoidably, other sacrifices would have to follow. As usual, she pushed her principle to its extreme, regardless of the danger that the "generalized non-intervention" could lead to a generalized enslavement.

The surrender of Czechoslovakia to Germany was obligatory from this viewpoint. Certainly, "a German hegemony" was "stifling," but this was also supposed to be in the interest of the current condition of peace.[102] Sophisms served to blur the difference between democracy and dictatorship, between the French Republic and German tyranny. Would a German hegemony be worse than a French one? In three decades would Germany be a democracy and France a dictatorship? These were idle speculations which one could consider cynical if one were not familiar with their author's proverbial sincerity and her tendency toward a stubborn, even reckless consistency. This behavior is known to us from the beginning: she always went uncompromisingly to the utmost extreme, never stopping halfway.

Added to these speculations were a few more. As a pacifist, she gave voice to the idea that France's "spiritual radiance" would be able to grow in spite of the surrender to Hitler. Moreover, she held that up until this point every hegemony had weakened the victorious state—a doubtful thesis against which numerous historical proofs can be found. She felt it would be "true progress" when the German annexation of Czechoslovakia brought about such a peaceful process.[103] These were unrealistic notions which ignored the essence of totalitarianism, which by 1934 Simone Weil had already depicted so masterfully. In pacifistic circles, false hopes of this type circulated, only their propagandists did not always have the same sincere naivete. Among those acting in good faith were agents, controlled by the Nazis who were fishing in troubled waters. In 1940, the number of pacifists who were involved in collaboration was in no way small.

In a letter from 1938 addressed to Gaston Bergery, a spokesman for pacifism and a future ambassador under Pétain, Simone Weil pleaded for non-resistance to Germany,

stating her willingness to endure "a temporary state of vas-
salage." Proceeding still further, she would even accept
"exceptional laws" against Communists and Jews: "In my eyes
and probably in the eyes of most Frenchmen, this would be
fairly inconsequential. One can well imagine that nothing
essential would be affected..."[104] Finally, one could devote oneself to serious problems, like the construction of housing, the
"dignity of the workers," the spreading of the "wealth of art,
science, thought and other peaceful activities." All of this was
supposed to happen in a France under Hitler's dictatorship.

Her self-deception could not have been greater. One must
declare with dismay that this philosopher was now ready to
surrender those human values for which she had fought for
so long. For the sake of the preservation of peace, she wanted
to subject herself to German domination and sanction an
authoritarian regime which indulged in political and racist
persecution. Her theses resembled the agenda of the Pétain
dictatorship in 1940 and, therefore, her attitude toward the
new state was not viewed without sympathy. The renunciation of parliamentary democracy was easier for her since she
had always held such a system in contempt.

During 1939 new tendencies in her thought gradually
begin to stand out. The word "nation," she writes, implies an
"inexhaustible wealth" once more: the idea that destruction
threatens great nations is no longer a vision. Her *Réflexions
en Vue d'un Bilan*, written in March, is not concerned with the
maintenance of peace, but rather with war alone.[105] As there
was no longer any reason to speak of peace, the only realistic perspective would be that of "unlimited war." The preservation of one's own nation and the destruction of the enemy's
formed the object of the conflict. Yet such an aim would not
be likely to establish peace, rather it would give rise to new
conflicts.

The author of these remarks recognizes no essential difference between democracies and totalitarian states and

refuses to tie herself to the war aims of one or the other coalition. In order to be believable, the democracies would have to rigorously demonstrate their genuine commitment to their principles because, since 1914, she had taken note of "an unpleasant hypocrisy among them." France would have to resemble a "constantly bubbling source of freedom." All freedom-loving human beings would take pleasure in France's existence. Since this was not the case, it would have to be worked on. In view of the very real danger of war, this was a truly abstract project with echoes of an earlier theme. Indeed, a new direction is already announcing itself—the will to make the fatherland lovable with the intention of defending it. These reflections create the impression of a transitional phase, while a precise viewpoint is lacking. Although still vacillating, she was nonetheless ready to plunge herself into a dangerous situation. After the German occupiers put down a student protest in Prague, Simone Weil drafted a plan that used paratroopers to aid the population. "She explained her plan to different individuals and added that she would absolutely want to take part in the action. She vowed to throw herself under a bus if one put the plan into action without her."[106]

Here again, her striving announced itself. She would not stop at mere words, but had to take an action which demanded the greatest sacrifice. Nothing would come of this. An airplane specialist had told her, "all the people whom you want to help will die doing this." To which she provided the cutting rejoinder, "good, they will die, but they will die with dignity." Morality takes precedence over love of one's fellow man. The ethical dictate reveals extreme cold-heartedness— very much in the Kantian sense. The whole thing was intended less to help others than to prove herself. The altruism veiled a strong, egocentric need. More than anything else she sought her own sacrifice.

Her view could have stood under the motto "neither war nor peace." Her interest in the realization of domestic political reforms took priority. But this meant sticking her head in the sand and looking away from the impending danger of war. Illusory constructions took the place of analytical, incisive thinking; flagrant contradictions became evident.

While Simone Weil called Nazi Germany, "a country stretched to the utmost" and characterized Hitler, obsessed with the "Wagnerian aesthetic," as a human being whom no "human consideration" would be able to stop, she again comforted herself with the dream that Germany was on the verge of weakening itself and losing the "unusual submissiveness of its workers." She wavered between the realistic projection of an "unlimited war" and the illusory hope that everything still could turn out for the best.

Her distance from the democratic states sprang from the social-revolutionary struggle which had been conducted for years. The degradation of the poor, the contempt for the workers could not be forgotten. Yet most unbearable was the disgrace of the colonial system. Solidarity with those peoples under the rule of France was a persistent concern. In 1930 an uprising in Vietnam aroused her awareness of colonial injustice:

> Since that day, I am ashamed of my country. Since that day, I am unable to meet an Indochinese, an Algerian or a Moroccan without asking for forgiveness. Forgiveness for all of the pains, all of the humiliations which are being done to him, to his people. For their oppressor is the French state which acts in the name of all French people; accordingly, if to a lesser extent, even in my own name. Therefore, in view of those oppressed by France, I must be ashamed and feel the need to atone for mistakes.[107]

In November, 1939, after the outbreak of war, she writes to Jean Giraudoux, the government's Information Deputy, that she "cannot believe that France's cause is just, because of the colonies."[108] Again and again the same attitude:

Simone Weil feels personally responsible for social injustice. She never tried to make an excuse to evade her responsibility. The exploitation of the workers concerned her as directly as the oppression of the colonized. In every single case, she identified herself with the down-trodden and tried to be one of them—which was difficult and frequently proved unsuccessful.

First France's collapse in June, 1940 caused an intellectual turning point. The philosopher abandoned pacifism and found her way to resistance against victorious Germany. Thus she designed the plan for a troop of nurses who were supposed to be sent to the front lines. A text from those days opened in a very militaristic way: "One requires no tank or airplane to kill a human being. A kitchen knife suffices. If all those who are disgusted with the Nazi executioners rise up together and the armed forces strike the decisive blow, liberation will quickly ensue."[109] Yet, according to her, one would have to reckon with a waiting period of long years, not sacrificing human lives prematurely, arming for the struggle: "Everyone must know that he has the duty to one day participate in the struggle, and that he must be ready." In this struggle, a new society would arise "based on generosity and co-operation."

It is the old ideal of the community of solidarity. That which at one time the Anarchist-Syndicalists should have realized, now was expected from resistance to the totalitarian oppression. Yet the situation was not the same; all the factors had changed. The order of the day was not the liberation of workers from capitalism, but rather the liberation of the French nation from German oppression. The difference was not perceived clearly at first; old and new notions came together in a confused fashion. Soon, however, the change became apparent. Simone Weil rid herself of her pacifism and now supported the energetic conduct of war with the same passion. Her assessment of the personified value of France is new. We know that this philosopher had viewed France very skeptically. Her country, imperiled by the military defeat, now appears to her in a new light. Simone Weil was mindful of "the precious things which we have lost because we did not know to value them, the things which we reconquer, whose price we now comprehend, we must preserve."

One could also understand such remarks as an expression of self-criticism. Looking back, in London in 1943, Simone Weil, this resister, called her pacifistic view a "criminal error" which had been fostered by poor health. She had, consequently, failed to recognize the "tendency toward betrayal" in the pacifistic circles.[110]

CHAPTER

8

GOD'S LOVE

Simone Weil's turn toward religion can be dated precisely—
it results from the collapse of her revolutionary hopes. By
1934 she had proclaimed: "From human beings, no help can
be expected."

Her disappointing experience in the Spanish Civil War
ultimately led to her renunciation of the social-revolutionary
world-view. In 1937, when the injury to her leg was partially
healed and she was on vacation from teaching, she traveled
to Italy for the first time. Rome, Assisi, Florence—the country
and its people charmed her. She attended Whitsuntide Mass
in St. Peter's Cathedral. In the museums, she most admired
the Greek statues, Umbria appeared as the height of beauty.
To her parents she wrote:

> Never would I have dreamt of such a landscape, of such a
> charming sort of people, of such impressive churches...
> Everything in Assisi is Franciscan and everywhere, in addition,
> are examples of what has been done to honor Saint
> Francis...One could believe that Providence had created these
> smiling fields and these touchingly humble chapels as prepa-
> ration for his coming...When I was alone in the small Roman
> chapel from the twelfth century, Santa Maria degli Angeli, this

incomparable miracle of purity where Saint Francis prayed so often, for the first time in my life something that was stronger than I was forced me to my knees.[111]

On the continuation of the journey, she enjoyed Florence, the museums and churches, and above all, music: Mozart's *Marriage of Figaro* and especially Monteverdi's *Coronation of Poppea*.

She passionately admired beauty as the supreme thing on earth, as the symbol of God. "God is truly present in everything which awakens the pure and authentic feeling of the beautiful in us. It is as though there is an incarnation of God in the world whose manifestation is beauty...The beautiful is something on which one's attention can dwell."[112] She saw the culmination of beauty in Gregorian music. Even more perfect than Bach and Mozart, it was "like all great art, equal amounts of pure technique and pure love." Conscious of the distortions and perversions of art, she states: "For that reason, all art of the highest quality is, according to its essence, religious art (something which one no longer knows these days.) A Gregorian melody is just as much a testimonial as the death of a martyr."[113] Moreover, she believed that contemporary art had no future "because all art is collective and there no longer is a collective life (there are only collectives which remain dead) and because the true alliance between body and soul is broken...It is therefore completely futile for you to envy Leonardo da Vinci or Bach. The great ones of our age have taken another path."[114] Art would be "reborn from the womb of great anarchy." This could "only be lonely, hidden in the dark and without an echo." Simone Weil was so filled by that type of aesthetic longing that she once mentioned the wish to retire to Venice and just listen to music.

During Holy Week in 1938, she had intense religious experiences in the Benedictine Abbey at Solesmes: "I had throbbing headaches. Every sound hurt me like a blow. Then I made an extreme effort to concentrate, to step out of this miserable flesh, to send it cowering alone into its corner and find a pure and perfect joy in the unprecedented beauty of the music and words. Thanks to this experience, I am trying, with the help of analogous arguments, to better understand the possibility of loving the divine love through misery. Of course, Christ's passion did not enter me once and for all during that mass."[115]

In Solesmes she met a young Englishman who "brought her to understand for the first time the idea of the miraculous power of the sacrament through the truly angelic transfiguration which enveloped him after Communion." Thus she came to know the mystic thinkers of the seventeenth century, among them, George Herbert, whose poem "Love" made the strongest impression. God is the love which receives the sinner and forgives him:

Sit! He whoever tastes of my flesh, he recovers—
So I then sat myself down at the table—and ate.

Simone Weil perceived these verses as a simultaneous spiritual and physical occurrence "amid pain, the presence of love, as one feels it in the smile on a beloved face." After constantly repressing her libidinous drives and denying her feminine nature, she seized upon religion above all as a precept of love. One must interpret this as a form of sublimated eroticism. In "Love," love is equated with the flesh, of which the guest partakes. Simone Weil always had difficulties eating; she ate as little as possible. The nourishment to which she attached the greatest worth was of the intellectual type. The spiritual bread becomes increasingly more momentous; hunger, a principle of the highest moral value. Reciting the admired poem, she had the sensation: "Christ Himself rose up and took hold of me." A parable elucidates the incident:

He entered my room and said: "Miseries, which you do not understand, which you do not know. Come with me and I will teach you things, which you never suspected." I followed him...Sometimes he was silent, took bread from the cupboard, and we shared it. This bread had the taste of real bread. Never again should I know the same taste. In my glass and in his he poured wine, which smelled of the sun and the earth on which the city was built. Sometimes we stretched ourselves out on the floor of the attic and the ecstacy of sleep lowered itself onto me. Then I awoke and drank in the sunlight. One day he said to me: "And now, go!" I fell to the floor, embraced his knees and beseeched him not to send me away![116]

In such experiences, God is experienced sensuously. One knows it from the experiments of all the mystics, from the prophets, Buddha and Jesus, to Teresa of Avila. Here, Simone Weil experiences that happiness which, until this point, she had sought in vain, which solidarity with revolutionaries and friendship with humans had not provided to her. She is also aware of one of the sources of her own thoughts: "Human sexual energy is not restricted by season. The best evidence for that is that it is not intended for any practical purpose, but rather for God's love."[117] After failed experiments, Simone Weil's libido finds fulfillment in the mystical sight of God, in personal effacement in favor of merging with the love object.

Before her departure from Marseilles in May, 1942, she sent a *Spiritual Autobiography* to the Dominican prior Jean-Marie Perrin, with whom she had held long, intensive discussions about religious problems. In this thorough text, the nearness to Christ was described, as well as her distance from the Church. Simone Weil movingly declared her gratitude for the proffered friendship, the likes of which she had never known before. Yet despite the intimacy of the spiritual relationship, she had refused baptism. She felt that she belonged to Christianity, yet not to the Church: "not one single time, not once for a second, did I have the feeling that God would want me in the Church."[118]

Given its demands, Catholicism appeared universally restrictive to her, excluding manifold things. "So many things remain outside of its horizon, so many things that I love and do not want to give up; so many things, which God loves because otherwise they would not exist: the vast dimension of the past centuries, with the exception of the last twenty years; all countries inhabited by colored races; the entire secular life of the countries of the white race, everyone there guilty of heresy against the traditions, like those of the Manicheists and Albigenses; all the creations of the Renaissance, which are not completely worthless, even if they are often disparaged."[119]

She emphasized her personal views, her knowledge—which she did not want to renounce. Her distance from the Church became clear. In addition, her interpretation of Christianity transcended all norms. Christ lost his uniqueness in favor of God who was already present in the earlier religions like Buddhism. With her usual energy, she defended her conviction. To the prior she wrote: "I have resisted you constantly."

She was of the opinion that her position stood in harmony with God's will: "I believe that now finally one can conclude that God does not want to have me in the Church." The demand to assimilate the entire history of the world, all cultures and races, was heretical in nature and approached the theories of Teilhard de Chardins. The Church was reproached with "misuse of power." It would have to acknowledge "that it has changed or wants to change. How else could one take the Church seriously when one remembers the Inquisition?"[120] The Catholic Church has a totalitarian character: "After the fall of the Roman Empire, which had been totalitarian, the Church established totalitarianism in the thirteenth century after the Albigense War. This tree bore considerable fruit."[121] Between this philosopher and the Church stood insurmountable obstacles which could never be cleared away. Simone Weil's sympathies belonged to the heretics. She had always acted as a heretic, and she continued to act in this way. As usual, when she felt pressure to steer her in a direction other than the one she herself had determined, her opposition grew.

Never before had she written so thoroughly and passionately. The shyness, which was characteristic of her, had always imposed a reserve on her. Here the intimate relationship with Father Perrin, the past discussions about the basic questions of existence and, finally, the notion of an ultimate demise had their effect.

Consequently, she wrote: "I would like to speak to you once more before my departure, perhaps for the last time..."[122] She described her state of mind in this way: "persistent sorrow is my fate. Even with the most strenuous concentration the greatest and purest joys makes only a superficial impression on me. My sorrow issues from my pitiful and constant sins, and, ultimately, from all of the misery of our age and the past centuries."[123] Not even religious faith provided any solace, any reconciliation, to this tormented thinker. The most extreme anxiety remained. It could not be otherwise in view of her perception of the continuing injustice, which she felt as an intense pain.

The criticism of the societal function of the Church provides evidence that the meaning of this life continues to receive her attention. Simone Weil is still reflecting on how to create a more habitable, more humane world. In a second letter addressed to Father Perrin from Casablanca on May 26, 1942, the criticism of the Church as an "earthly fatherland" is repeated. A few of Perrin's statements even cause her to charge him with "a serious defect," he remained rooted in a dogmatic pretension to truth.

In contrast, she sets her own conviction: "God's children can have no other fatherland here on earth than the universe with all of the rational creatures who have populated, populate, and will populate it. It is the home which has claim on our love."[124] The Church cannot lay such a claim; its dogmas are in opposition to the world. This philosopher declares her allegiance to an entire universe of indiscriminately encompassing love: "Our love must fill the collective space to the same extent, with the same intensity, as sunlight." This omnipresent love is also characteristic of "a solid covering of protective indifference from a distance."[125] No room is left for emotions; friendship is permitted as an exception, but within limits. Nothing should distract from the universal command. In the present, universality is more imperative than ever: "It must influence language and all conduct." A "new saintliness" was necessary: "It just does not mean anything today to be a saint. A saintliness is required; the present moment demands it, a new, until now unknown saintliness...The world requires saints replete with genius, just as a city ravaged by the plague requires doctors."[126]

She did not feel herself called to this; she was "considerably defective," a "ruined instrument," and also "too exhausted." In view of such failings, she had "more to fear from God's wrath than many great criminals." Yet, she added, in reality she did not fear that wrath; indeed, she even loved it. What she feared was something else: "It is the thought of God's possible kindness, his mercy, which evokes a kind of fear in me, which makes me tremble."[127] Nonetheless, at the same time, she also believed that she was proclaiming truth, carrying something within herself which was ultimately more valuable than she herself. In this we are witnessing a dual occurrence, an abasement as well as an exaltation. This combination of opposites was always present in the character of this philosopher.

Above all, Simone Weil's religious concept was devoted to actual existence. The commandment to love was supposed to satisfy human beings and endow their lives with meaning. This corresponded to her old aim of liberating the oppressed:

"Exactly as God is powerless to do good among human beings without their co-operation, the same goes for the Devil in the realization of evil."[128]

What Simone Weil connects pre-eminently with the world is aesthetic meaning whose pinnacle, for her, was the Greek tradition. Depth of spirit and beauty of form are identical. Plato is true as well as beautiful, as is Homer: "In this life, there is actually only one single beauty; this is the beauty of the world. The other beauties are only its reflection, either great and pure or distorted and defiled or even diabolically perverted."[129] Beauty was expressed most beautifully in antiquity, in Greece, China and India. "The Greek Stoicism, something wondrous and very close to early Christianity, especially to the thoughts of Saint John, was almost exclusively love of worldly beauty."

Another rare belief is expressed in this statement: "What pertains to Israel, some passages from the Old Testament—the Psalms, the Book of Job, Isaiah, the Proverbs—is an incomparable glorification of worldly beauty."[130] She held that there were analogies between Francis of Assisi and John of the Cross. But in general one could say that "the world's beauty" has "no place in the Christian tradition." This is strange, the reason, hardly understandable. It is a terrible void. How could Christianity claim to call itself catholic when the universe is excluded from it? The Renaissance had not found the true path to antiquity. "Today one could believe that the white race has lost its feeling for the beauty in the world and pursues the task of banishing this meaning from all parts of the earth which it subjugates with its weapons, its trade and its religion."[131]

Here the distance from ascetic Judaism and Protestantism, with their antagonism to images, is revealed. Simone Weil's aesthetic desire found instead a certain satisfaction in the ceremonies, architecture and music of the Catholic Church. At this point a motif is evident: she has alienated herself from those religions, which, in many matters, were closely associated with her.

Only once, after the "Greek wonder," did Simone Weil discover an exemplary civilization whose value she sought to illuminate: the occidental culture of the twelfth century in southwest France. The Catharists ("the pure ones") had accepted Near Eastern ideas, which, in the wake of the crusades, achieved dissemination and led to the schism. The heretics rebelled against the depravity of the Church and abandoned themselves to asceticism. They advocated a Manicheistic doctrine which equated this life with evil. Moreover, they were non-violent and averse to all dogma. There she found kindred ideas, a last flash of Greek antiquity: "As little as one knows about the Catharists, it seems nonetheless clear that they were somehow heirs to Platonic thought, to secret cults and mysteries of that pre-Roman civilization which included the Mediterranean and the Near East. As it happens, some aspects of their doctrine refer to Buddhism, to Pythagoras, to Plato as well as to the Druid doctrine which had left its mark on the same ground."[132] The Catharists are the model for synchretism, as it corresponds to Simone Weil's thought. There, too, she finds a role model for political organization. For a long time, the Occitanian provinces, with the cities Toulouse, Albi, Avignon and Marseilles, fostered a pronounced spirit of tolerance. Their structures were decentralized. "The unification of this spirit with the public spirit, an affection for freedom as lively as that for the legitimacy of the feudal lords, one has probably not seen this anywhere else as it was in the Occital of the twelfth century."[133] She sees in this a model for balance, for an equilibrium between various factors, between city and country, between freedom and authority. "More than two centuries before Joan of Arc, the feeling for the fatherland—a fatherland which of course was not France—was the main motive of those people and they already had a word to des-

ignate the fatherland, they called it language."[134] The freedom
movement of the "pure ones" was cruelly subdued by a coalition of the popes and the French royalty. The Catharists were
tortured and killed en masse; their cities, plundered and
destroyed. With harsh words, she condemned the "perfidy"
of the Church which had destroyed a humane civilization.
Published in the *Cahiers du Sud* in 1943, she hoped that more
than her two essays would keep the memory of this civilization alive. In the lost Occitan there were "longings which have
not yet disappeared and which we cannot allow to disappear
even when we cannot hope to fulfill them."[135] Civilizations are
mortal. Simone Weil knew this as well as Paul Valéry did.
Forgetting their mortality meant slaying the victims once
more. "One kills a second time what has been destroyed. One
participates in the horror of the weapons." The remembrance
of evil is supposed to help uncover the sources of good.

Momentous reasons prevented her from converting to
Catholicism. She claimed to be without as well as within the
Church, to be more exact, "on the threshold." The distance
remained in existence, nonetheless, until the end. In 1942 she
wrote, "insurmountable difficulties of a philosophical nature"
made this necessary. It would not be the mysteries themselves, "but rather the adornments with which the Church
believed it had to surround them, especially the well-known
use of the words *anathema sit*."[136] Her criticism of the authoritarian spirit of the Roman hierarchy persisted with undi-
minished sharpness. The development from Catholic to
modern totalitarianism was interpreted as a further decline:
"With every about-face, humanity sinks deeper. How far will
it go?"[137]

Certainly this is no thorough analysis of Church history,
rather it is a criticism of the moment. Simone Weil's views
indicate her distance from Catholicism on principle. Her synchretism, which combined aspects of numerous religions, is
not compatible with any church dogma. In this, a very per-

sonal interpretation becomes apparent, and she feared, not unjustly, that Father Perrin would conclude from her interpretation, "satanic arrogance."

In Marseilles, where she primarily stayed from October, 1940 until May, 1942, she was associated with Father Chaillet's resistance group, *Témoignage Chrétian*; with the newly founded journal, *Les Cahiers du Sud*; and with the Catholic worker youth group, J.O.C. In early 1941 she was interrogated by the French police repeatedly. She became acquainted with the poet Joë Bousquet, who, due to an injury in the First World War, was confined to bed. Their spiritual connection became very close. Simone Weil even alluded to her mystical experiences, about which she was usually silent. During Holy Week in 1942, she took part in masses at the Benedictine abbey, El Calcat, in Dourgnes. The discussions with Jean-Marie Perrin, the prior of the Dominicans in Marseilles, left a great impression. While visiting she participated in debates in the cloister and gave lectures about Greek and Hindu philosophy since she was then studying the Bhagavad-Gita and Sanskrit.

She tried hard to find further employment in the teaching profession from which she was excluded due to the race legislation. In a letter from October 18, 1941, to the Commissioner for Jewish Affairs, she wrote that she "had never considered herself a Jew, was never in a synagogue, [came] from parents who were freethinkers, was raised in a thoroughly nonreligious manner..."[138] Feeling no solidarity with the persecuted Jews, she insisted on her individuality as well as on her relationship to French society, which, in the same breath, affirmed Christian values and organized the discrimination against the Jews. Indeed, in her letter, she even thanked the government for excluding her from the category of intellectuals since this gave her the opportunity to perform practical labor. True to her habit, she had thrown herself into manual work and had helped with the grape harvest for a few weeks. She writes:

Only he whose daily exhaustion painfully twists his limbs possesses the earth and nature. Only he who struggles from sun-
rise to sunset in the agony of a fatigue which accumulates as
it is renewed daily, only to him do the days, months, years,
seasons and the indefatigable circle of the vault of heaven
belong. Only he attends the orbit of the stars; only he lives the
days and does not dream them. The government, which acts
on my behalf, has given me all that. It, and the other current
rulers of our country, have given me what they themselves do
not possess. They have intended another unending gift for me,
which likewise even they do not possess: the gift of poverty.[139]

Actually, the Petain regime had extolled farming and the
sacredness of the earth and had attributed France's defeat to
the corruption of the cities. Such ideas were not unfamiliar to
her. Certainly, her letter to the governmental representative
had ironic undertones, yet the truth of her conviction did not
manifest itself any less.

She worked on the farm of Gustave Thibon, a farmer and
religious philosopher. There she spent a month cutting
grapes. There, too, she perceived the work as torment and
release at the same time—similar to her experience in the factory. Again she wore herself out to the point of exhaustion.
The vine-grower reports:

She was successful in working exactly as much as the other
workers. One could certainly see that she was exhausted
sometimes—but she did not relent...Her unparalleled personal will made her want to accomplish every task: milking
the cows in the morning, drying the dishes in the evening and
cleaning the vegetables...One always had to force her to eat
regularly, for if it had been left to her, she would have only
eaten onions and tomatoes—insufficient nourishment. In
terms of her health, this experience was quite bad for her. She
suffered frequently from headaches.[140]

At night she wrote her texts and letters. She experienced
the labor as a passion full of pain and happiness. To Gustave

Thibon she confided her feeling of being dead and in Hell, damned to cut grapes for eternity. With Thibon, whom she had come to know through Father Perrin, she had long discussions which became increasingly prolonged as their different viewpoints clashed.

During that time, she devoted herself to a Spanish militiaman who was imprisoned in a French internment camp and completely forsaken. A correspondence ensued and packages were sent to the camp. Fruitless efforts were made to obtain his release. In Antonio, this simple man of the people, she recognized stoic behavior. "Ultimately, I would like you to suffer no longer. I would like to be in your place, and you in mine."[140]

CHAPTER

9

THE VOID

Against the backdrop of "indifference" praised by Simone Weil, she began to appear increasingly hardhearted. Association with her—never easy—became still more difficult. Thibon notes: "She showed her unpleasant side which was unrestrained and reckless. Indeed, a lot of the time, affection and forbearance was required until the best in her ventured into the light."[142]

The poet Jean Tortel, a colleague at *Cahiers du Sud,* also described the unusualness and difficulty of an encounter with her:

> ...strange and perhaps incomprehensible...unknown among us, a bit terrifying (a bit terrible), at first glance, extremely ugly. A thin face, made conspicuous by her large, black, Basque cap, from which stiff hair stood out. An invisible body, since the cape only allowed rough, black shoes to be seen. She looked—when she did look—through glasses, the eyes well forward, but the head and upper body were also inclined (due to her strong near-sightedness) with an intensity and questioning eagerness, which I found nowhere else...Her presence ruled out every 'lie,' but at times I felt a sort of need to avoid this revealing, disruptive glance. This glance, itself confused, took hold and left him who met it, bare.[143]

The extremely depressing atmosphere and the relent-
lessness revealed in this portrait were not born easily by
others. She had always been inflexible in her convictions and
remained so until the end. (However, Simone Pétrement
declared that her friend later became "milder.")[144]

A visit to former fellow students in Carcassonne left
behind a similarly odd impression. "I want to serve," she
said, "I want to go where it is the most dangerous...where my
life is the most exposed." Jacques Cabaud reports: "When she
left, an oppressive atmosphere remained. It affected all of
those present. Her peculiar appearance and her remoteness
from things temporal, from the problems of the here and now,
had even made an impression on Jean Paulhan,* who spent
the evening with us."[145]

Her moral severity led to extreme harshness in her living
style. For Simone Weil it was natural to be satisfied with the
official food ration, and she wanted everyone else to be satisfied with it. In her eyes, those who disapproved of the political concepts of the government nonetheless owed it
obedience in all other areas. Therefore, in a letter to
American Ambassador Leahy, she asked that the United
States halt wheat deliveries to France. According to her, since
most Frenchmen were supporters of de Gaulle, they would
have no right "to accept material offers from a government
which they rejected on principle." Moreover, she held that
Great Britain had to have priority. Finally, France must not be
granted any help as long as "shameful things" were happen-
ing in the concentration camps.[146] In similar fashion, she
turned her criticism against a Leftist politician who, in order
to escape arrest, had claimed the aid of the Dominicans: "You
have no right to accept help from those whose beliefs you
spurn."[147] Dogmatic severity limited her Christian charity

---

*As one of the managers of Gallimard Publishing, Jean Paulhan exercised
a significant literary influence.

which deliberately subjected everything to her characteristically rigid standards.

Denying any link to the oppressed Jews was typical of her. This attitude was particularly striking since she exhibited understanding for the oppressed of every nation and of every faith—with the exception of the Jews. She substantiated her antipathy with Biblical history, which she interpreted in a one-sided manner. Israel, exactly like Rome, served as a symbol of the "great beast," of material power. "Israel has chosen the national God as well as denied Christ the mediator...Israel's malediction weighs upon Christianity."[148] She held it responsible for all monstrous crimes—the Inquisition, the persecution of heretics, totalitarianism. As Christ's executioners, the Jews, "this handful of uprooted people," had brought about "all of the uprooting on earth." This monocausal model supported the themes which the fascist dictators popularized for the justification of genocide. The manicheistic simplification, which projected everything evil onto a people, was not merely false—it relied on arguments which legitimized one of the worst crimes in history.

So often those passionately engaged in the struggle against injustice have a fatal flaw whereby an aspect of their thinking, such as a truly mathematical logic, is pushed to an extreme, to conclusions which can lead ultimately to the inhuman. It is significant that the German edition of *Gravity and Grace* forgoes the printing of these dismaying passages from the French original. This is a dubious attempt to serve the idealization of Simone Weil. But the authenticity of this excerpt remains. As distressing as her anti-semitism might be, it belongs to her philosophy. Well-meaning revisions only produce a false image. Ultimately, the sharp turning away from Judaism was not supposed to express the personal nature of an existential decision. Simone Weil did not want to share the fate which had been forced on the Jews; rather she insisted on determining her own fate. This is in complete contradiction with her resolution: "To emerge from oneself means total renunciation of being someone, the complete consent just to be something."[149] Here a totally vehement self-confidence confronts us. This path of renunciation was trying. It could only be a persistent struggle against oneself, a breaking of one's will and, lastly, self-effacement. Only in misery, was God's love supposed to manifest itself. As a result of this, one would have to endure misery gladly and not resist it. The mysticism of suffering prevented a real bond with those who were miserable. Ultimately, it refers to an exclusively personal experience. Still more resolved, Simone Weil went her way alone. She only entrusted her intimate thoughts and mystical experiences to paper, without a thought to publication.

Above all, these views radically changed her concept of freedom which previously had determined her entire way of thinking. It was now taken over by the concept of obedience. In her *Autobiography of the Spiritual* she writes that it is necessary to follow a strong impulse which has nothing in common with reason: "In this way, I understand obedience. I tested this conception when I went into the factory and stayed there while being in a state of intense and constant pain, as I recently described it. That life, in which everything is determined by the force of circumstances or impulses, and the possibility of choice does not exist, always appeared to me as the most beautiful."[150]

This religious determinism is of course the antithesis of the formerly advocated philosophy with its central requisite of free will. In that philosophy, the loss of one's personal will was considered the worst misery which can befall a human being. Now the assumptions are inverted: "It is my greatest wish to lose not only all personal will, but also all personal substance."[151] The goal remained unattainable. It could hardly be otherwise. The wish to free herself from personal will, to be only an instrument of divine power, was based on a self-deception; this is always the case with founders of religion and with prophets. The powerful strength of will which Simone Weil had always demonstrated did not stop determining her behavior. Until the end, she made her decisions with relentless energy.

The glorification of the world was replaced by a gloom which revealed the void. The world is the sphere of evil; God is not present in it: "The absence of God is the most wondrous evidence of his perfect love..."[152] It is no longer valid to safeguard the universe, to let justice hold sway. "Fell the tree and its own dead body shall be the fruit. Pluck out the vegetative energy."[153] God is absent; the omnipresent void, liberation. "We must arrive at the end of our existence in order to understand the concept of no longer being."[154] Simone Weil sought emptiness as release:

> Emptying out of desires, of the striving for substantive goals, vacant, resigned longing. Loose our desire for all goods and wait. Experience proves that this waiting finds fulfillment. Then one touches the absolute good. All in all, [it is] beyond anything extraordinary, which it also might be, [this] being of non-existent will, wanting the void...But this void is fuller than any fullness.[155]

According to the model of Buddhism, "the effacement of desires" as well as resistance to all temptations, is sought to supplant the void: "Reject every belief which fills up the empty spaces, which is supposed to ease the bitterness. That [belief] in immortality. That [belief] in the usefulness of sins: *etiam peccata.* That [belief] in a certain ordering of events through providence—in short: [reject] the comforts which one usually seeks in religion."[156] The void is the only reality. To become conscious of it, to love the void, to be nothing, is the pressing task. The world has stopped being identical with beauty. The aesthetic has lost its charm and horror reigns. Any hope of liberation, which Christianity and Buddhism offer, is ruled out.

Simone Weil's belief conveys no peace, embodying far more an extreme disquiet. The void is not a constant factor. In view of the false hopes of religion, even atheism acquires a new worth: "Given two people without knowledge of God, it is he who denies him, who is perhaps closest to Him...Insofar as religion is a source of comfort, it is an obstacle to true belief. In this sense, atheism is a purging."[157]

Such statements cannot easily fit into the framework of a church. They particularly contradict the numerous comforts of Catholicism. Her personal belief—analogous to the existential view—abides in solitude and asserts itself against institutionalized rites and dogma. Hers is a type of anarchistic religiousness which continues the rebelliousness of the past. Such a view of faith, filled with anxiety and doubt, more closely resembles that of the Jews and Protestants than that of the Catholics. Yet this is hardly mentioned, much less perceived seriously. Her conception is monotheistic. Jesus is identical to God, never appearing as His son. The crucifixion is not the fulfillment of a mission, but rather the sheer expression of suffering. Jewish heritage stands out clearly here, above all in the last interpretation which depicts God as absent, invisible. According to Erich Fromm in, *You Will Be Like God*, negative theology in general is the quintessence of the Jewish religion, just as "not the right belief, but rather the right action" characterizes it.

The theological declarations carry absolutely personal attributes, signs of her own experience and her own thinking. One discovers a synchronism in the confluence of various religious and philosophical doctrines—Buddha and Jesus, Homer and Plato, Pascal and Kierkegaard. Without stressing a difference, Simone Weil cited Krishna and Jesus as witnesses to the same religion. The final form of her thought, the negative theology, emphatically refers to the Gnostics of the early Christian era and to the medieval Catharists. According to this conception, evil prevails in the world and it is forbidden to enter into compromises with it. "Goodness is impossible."[158] Therefore, one should endure evil and love suffering. "Nothing that exists is absolutely worthy of love. One has to love what does not exist."[159] One should "love being nothing," understand death as union with God and, lastly, love evil because it is "the shadow of good." No reference is needed to the foundation of disillusionment and despair on which such negation was based. How much love changed into rejection and hate there!

Mystics were always alienated from the world and from human beings. Their actions were an expression of extreme subjectivity. In their thoughts they were close to death and sought their end through hunger and flagellation. They mistrusted church institutions. Loners and rebels, they were fascinated by their own personal redemption, less by that of human beings in general. These are attitudes which are also significant for this French thinker. "Desire nothing but the cross and, moreover, without solace, for that is perfect," promised John of the Cross, for whom "misery, extending until the very last," had "an irresistible attraction."[160] This Spanish monk was thrown into prison as a rebel by his own Carmelite order because he had independently introduced strict rules. He posited his mystical ecstacy against the general duties. With John of the Cross, as with other mystics, one finds the expression of erotic longings in religious garb:

And among sacred kisses
I swore an oath to Him,
to be with Him eternally.

A great spiritual wave extends itself from the Christian mystics Johannes Scotus Erigena, Meister Eckhart and Jakob Béhme to Simone Weil. When Meister Eckhart postulates: "God is such a one whose nothingness fills the whole world; His something, however, is nowhere at all," the commonality of thought is evident. But there are still further analogies. Gershom Scholem has portrayed the ideas of the Jewish mystics, who made use of a greater leeway to indulge in their own speculations, as Catholic non-conformists: "The thesis of God as a pure nothingness was advocated by thirteenth century Spanish Cabalists without any authority having taken action against them."[161] This is not mentioned by Simone Weil. It is not known how much she knew about it or whether she repressed it.

With her negative theology, she belongs in the succession of mystical faithful. Of course she too was unable to attain the goal sought by them: "Fervent attitude—I must necessarily turn to something other than myself, as it is a question of being freed from oneself."[162] It is exactly this which the mystical course is unable to attain because it requires the greatest concentration on the person himself. The desired liberation from the subject generally means liberation from life, affirmation of death as the realization of real life.

Karl Jaspers comments on this: "There are great seductions—to deprive a human being of himself through belief in God, to justify his solitude through the alleged recognition of absolute truth, to provide him with supposed contentment through the possession of existence itself, which is truly inhumanity to man."[163] No one is more exposed to this danger than the mystic who thinks and interprets distinctly and individually. In no way, can one assert that Simone Weil has escaped from this danger. Disappointed by human beings and by life, she withdrew increasingly into herself, into the shell of her subjectivity. Yet the "contentment" cited by Jaspers can hardly apply to her, her thoughts were driven by turbulent restlessness until the end. But what cannot be overlooked is the estrangement from human beings, guided by the precept: "Killing everything that one loves through one's thought: [It is] the only way to die."[164] The will to negation is directed against life. It displays harshness, self-righteousness and a lack of humane feeling. It is the radical reversal of an earlier concept which sought a solution in community. Now it turns its attention to the individual, creating isolation and introversion. Union with God promises fulfillment, but the solution is synonymous with effacement, death. The will to self-destruction simply transforms itself into the will to destroy. Simultaneously, the aggressiveness which she turned against herself was also directed at others. In so doing, humane feelings ceased to exist. The spirit of this sentence is carried to the end: "No help is be expected from human beings." In addition, there is the certainty that no help can be expected from God.

CHAPTER

10

TAKING ROOT

A cursory explanation cannot do justice to Simone Weil's mental state. It was not continuously alienated from the world; negative theology and the mysticism of death were only one aspect of her world view; she was also a keen observer of society and closely watched its development. Simone Weil's thought process' operated on two levels, one public and one private, one socio-political and one mystical. No one could imagine the secret doctrine, its distance from her public reflections about society was too great.

She continued to occupy herself intensively with Plato and Hercules. At the center of her tragedy, *Venice Delivered*, which she started in 1940 but never completed, is the representation of a people threatened by ruin.* The outline refers to several historical facts. In 1618, Spain is supposed to have planned to take possession of Venice. The war plan was supposed to begin with the destruction of parts of the city. One of the conspirators—he is the hero of the piece—divulges the plan to the counsel and saves the city. The inference to the defeated France of that time is evident.

---

*Simone Weil barely knew about Hugo von Hoffmannsthal's drama of the same name, with a completely different plot, which was first staged in Berlin in 1905.

This maiden work reveals literary talent and makes refer-ence to classical models. Its author did not want to know about modern works. She sought her models elsewhere: "For the first time since Greece, let us resume the tradition of tragedy whose hero was perfect."[165] The play is a glorification of resistance, thematically related to Sartre's drama, *The Flies*, and Camus', *The Plague*. "Uprooting conquered peoples was always, and will always be, the politics of the conqueror. One must kill the city so that the citizens feel that not even a suc-cessful uprising could resurrect it. Then they will resign them-selves."[166] In the notes, the author writes about the hero of the play whose action saves Venice: "Perhaps one of the meanings of the passion is that the pain, the shame, the death, which one is unwilling to inflict upon others reverts to oneself, even when one has not wanted it to happen."[167] One is certainly jus-tified in viewing these thoughts as self-analysis. The following sentence also reveals a fundamental conviction: "One has to grant expression to the feeling that good is something abnor-mal. Actually, this is the case in this world."[168] The temporal struggle is fed by the transcendental belief.

One does not expect it to be otherwise. She was never sat-isfied with devising theories, always supplementing these with practical action. In Marseilles she took part in the first modest resistance groups which, nonetheless, could not sat-isfy her ambition. In vain she sought a way to London in order to be entrusted with a more active and—as she noted—preferably more dangerous mission by de Gaulle's command staff. When this was unsuccessful, she resolved to travel to the United States together with her parents, "who wished to escape the anti-semitism." For Simone Weil this was only a detour in order to attain her goal of getting to London. Hardly had she arrived in New York when she appealed to a former fellow-pupil of Alain's, Maurice Schumann, who held an important position on de Gaulle's staff. In a letter dated July 30, 1942, she urgently requested "support for her wish."[169]

For the majority of refugees, New York was the long desired asylum, a place of protection from hardships. This was not the case for this philosopher who suffered as though under a burden. She wrote that the departure from France had been terribly painful. It was only bearable "given the hope of assuming a greater and more active part in the efforts, dangers and suffering of this great struggle...Urgently, I ask for your support. I really believe that I can be useful. I appeal to you as a comrade to extricate me from this all too painful moral situation."

To Maurice Schumann she presented her plan for a "troop of nurses at the front" which she had previously submitted to the Ministry of War in May, 1940. Such a unit was supposed to be an example of the greatest courage. It's mission was to provide a different, yet counter-balancing, energy to the fighting spirit of the SS. The "moral vigilance of a symbol" was supposed to portray a different principle in the midst of general brutality. Once again Simone Weil's project failed. De Gaulle thrust it aside with the blunt response: "She is crazy."

Her actual, personal desire was, of course, to land with a parachute in occupied France to carry out acts of sabotage there. "Repeatedly I've had the opportunity to put my cold-bloodedness to the test in the face of immediate and deadly peril. I have stated that I possess the ability to perform under such circumstances. You know me well enough to know that I would not say this if it were not true. I would undertake a sabotage operation gladly. As for the communication of general instructions, I could do well at that since I just left France on May 14th and maintain contact with secret organizations."

With her usual persistence, she assailed her old school chum from Lycée Henri IV. She did not relent and vowed: "I cannot renounce trouble and danger due to my spiritual disposition. Fortunately, this is not the case for everyone, otherwise every organized action would be impossible. However, long experience has taught me that I can change nothing about my inclination. The widespread misery on the earth pursues and oppresses me so strongly that my powers are overcome. I am only able to find them once more and rid myself of this obsession when I myself assume a large part of the danger and suffering." This is a perfect self-portrait, which is not in need of commentary.

Maurice Schumann, radio announcer for *Free France* and later foreign minister, was successful in getting his comrade to England. On November 25, 1942, she arrived in Liverpool; on December 14, in London. However, the project, to be dispatched to occupied France, proved to be unworkable. The command of the Resistance considered Simone Weil unsuitable for such a complicated and dangerous operation. This plunged her, one resolved to do battle, into despair, for she wanted to take action and assume risk. Instead, she was put into a small office to check reports and programs which came out of France. While at this task, she used her time to write down some reflections. To her parents she communicated her regret at having left her home. She felt she would die of this despair. Nevertheless, one understands the decision of the Resistance leadership. Simone Weil would hardly have been capable of putting her plan into action. She would have put herself as well as others in danger. We know that she sought self-sacrifice, and this belongs, as always, in the sphere of personal decisions. When it concerns the fate of other human beings, this criterion is not sufficient. The personal decision must be judged against a collection of different factors.

Thus the young philosopher had spare time to devote herself to some reflections—her last ones. Only a few months more remained for her to live.

She wrote extremely productively and indefatigably in the same calm handwriting, without revisions and without expressing any nervousness. Her attention was aimed at the present, the war, but she was in the habit of incorporating past and future into her reflections. The present she characterized as being the result of a spiritual process; the triumphant totalitarianism, as the consequence of a moral and social decay. "This war is a war of religion."[170] She held that Europe could not be saved by the United States alone. That would put it at risk of falling prey to a "new bondage." She believed, "one has to remember that Europe was not subjugated by hordes who came from another continent or from the planet Mars, and that it is not sufficient to expel them. Europe suffers from an internal sickness. It requires a cure. Europe will only be able to live when it has liberated itself, for the most part, by itself." Required is the "fire of a true belief," because material weapons, airplanes and tanks are insufficient. There is reference to the necessity of respecting morality as the highest principle in the midst of a lethal struggle. In the course of the struggle, military strategists were increasingly inclined to forget this principle. Simone Weil expressed admiration for the English for their natural courage without loud bravado. This seemed exemplary to her and superior to the behavior of her own countrymen. She saw in this the "lively power of tradition" and proof "that some roots still draw their strength from a past filled with mystical light." It was plainly "supernatural" that the German forces had to halt at the English Channel.

In her writings from this time, religious creeds merge with shrewd social-political analyses which way makes it difficult to read her reflections. In the course of the war against Hitler's Germany, Europe would have to coalesce: "Similar to French unity, the achievement of European unity will be a compelling, vital, necessity in the very near future."[171] This unity would have to be forged during the struggle. Afterwards it would be more difficult, one had to assume the outbreak of civil wars. Spaniards, Italians, and anti-Nazi Germans were supposed to be incorporated into this united Europe: "The wave of hatred which will shake Europe after the German defeat is as great a moral danger as the wave of oppression in the year 1940."[172]

There were further reproaches, which went beyond the present day and were a mixture of sheer intelligence and dubious speculation. Her proposition, that Europe would have to liberate itself alone, was as well-intentioned as it was unrealistic. Without the contribution of the United States, the goal would never have been attained. However, the idea of European unification proved to be substantive and inspired.

The war appeared to her as a crisis of civilization which had produced almost analogous symptoms in the totalitarian and democratic states. Consequently, it would be of no value to re-establish the former state of affairs that had been eliminated by German authority. The basic evil she termed, "uprooting." Simone Weil's last reflections were directed at overcoming this sickness and uncovering the methods of "taking root." This would be a task of both a material and moral nature. The aim was the establishment of a balanced, unified society, as free of conflict as possible. The *Declaration of the Rights of Man* of 1789 should be replaced by a *Declaration of the Duties toward Man*. There were no rights without duties:

> The desires of the soul can be assigned, in most cases, to antitheses which balance and complete each other. The human soul requires equality and hierarchy...The human soul requires acquiescent obedience and freedom. The acquiescent obedience is that which is granted to an authority, considered to be legitimate. Such obedience is impossible vis-à-vis a power established by conquest or coup d'état or vis-à-vis an economic power based on money. The human soul requires truth and freedom of expression...The intellect must be able to express itself, without being restricted by any authority...The human soul requires solitude as well as life within society. The human soul requires personal possessions as it does social possessions...The human soul requires security and danger.[173]

To ensure intellectual freedom all propaganda should be forbidden; "protection from erroneous ideas and lies" should be guaranteed. Very dangerous ground is tread upon with the call for a ban on political parties—we consider this more closely later. Simone Weil set forth a series of dualities whose solution was supposed to result in a synthesis of freedom and obligation. Neither absolute state power nor absolute freedom is the solution, but rather the limitation of both with the aim of creating a balance. The inspiration of the Platonic vision of the state is recognizable here. The taking root should occur within "natural spheres" like fatherland, language, culture, profession and place of residence. The lack of such ties brought about the sickness of "uprooting."

In the winter of 1942-3, Simone Weil composed a comprehensive essay, *Taking Root*, as her contribution to the direction of the Resistance. It is a summary as well as an explanation of her ideas. The text of her counter-position to the *Declaration of the Rights of Man* from the French Revolution opens with this brazen tone: "The concept of obligation has priority over the concept of right[s]. This obligation is eternal."[174] She binds human beings to each other, leading them to a code of mutual respect. She draws this eternal law from religious testament. "The uprooting is by far the most dangerous sickness of human society because it reproduces itself."[175] Nothing, according to her, was more urgent than to counteract this sickness. France and Germany had succumbed to it in different ways: "In Germany, the uprooting had assumed the form of attack, while in France, it appeared in the shape of malaise and numbness."[176] It is a question of two forms of the same illness: "For that reason, one cannot assert that Hitler's victory over France in 1940 was the victory of a lie over truth. An incoherent lie has been defeated by a coherent one."[177]

In accordance with her usual methodology, Simone Weil addressed all societal problems according to an absolute principle. Consequently, liberalism seems as bad as racism; Marxism seems to be of the same substance as Hitlerism; the ideology of the French Revolution seems as destructive as modern totalitarianism. We are told that all of these concepts are lies created by science. All too numerous and varied phenomena are fused into the principle of evil which is confronted by an equally simple and uniform principle of good. The various forms and impulses of history force Simone Weil into a dualistic model. This was possible because she confronted history with a meta-historical criterion and nature, with a meta-natural one.

In her work one finds shrewd analyses of France, above all of its psyche and morals. Yet the back and forth movement between this world and the hereafter produced artificial solutions. She resumed ideas she formulated a decade earlier, her Marxist criticism. According to this, social problems could not be solved by nationalization. It would be necessary to adapt machines and industrial organizations to the workers. "Until now, the technicians have never considered anything other than the needs of production. If once they made a point of being mindful of the needs of the producers the entire production technology would undergo a gradual transformation."[178] Simone Weil pleaded for a decentralization of production and for the distribution of workshops throughout the entire country: "Such workshops would not be small factories. They would be industrial organisms of a new type in which a new spirit could reign. In spite of their small size they would be connected to each other by sufficiently strong, organic bonds to form a large-scale enterprise."[179]

Today such ideas are taken seriously. There are various attempts to translate them into reality. For Simone Weil, this industrial decentralization was supposed to bring nature closer and unite practical activity with theoretical instruction. Unmistakable here is an echo of the former anarchistic conviction. She praised the "great integrity" of that revolutionary movement and felt that one must "rediscover its tradition," without making an attempt to reawaken the movement.

Anarchistic spirit is also found in the very dubious call for the elimination of political parties. Simone Weil relies on Jean-Jacques Rousseau's concepts of direct democracy and attributes the downfall of the French Republic to the party system. Such criticism was popular at that time. It belonged to the ideology of the Pétain dictatorship and found an echo in some Resistance circles. Nevertheless, there was a spurious confusion between cause and effect. The political parties were less a cause than a reflection of the condition of society. It was an error to make the symptoms responsible for the disease.

She sought a liberal state without being capable of devising convincing structures. There is no example of a liberal system without parliamentary institutions and no example of parliamentary institutions without parties. The assertion that there were no parties in France in 1789 was totally false. Actually, political parties had emerged directly from the democratic revolt. That there are parties of very different quality is common knowledge—they correspond more or less to their mission. The ban on parties is simply an unsuitable means to an end. It does not represent the reform of democracy but rather its downfall. It is like the doctor who kills the patient in order to cure the disease.

The regime outlined actually possesses pronounced authoritarian characteristics, for it includes censorship, suppression of newspapers, monitoring of assembly and the death penalty. All of these things, naturally, were well-intended. Clearly, exactly these things often lead to intolerable excesses. One need only think about the monastic authority exercised by Savonarola in Florence or Robespierre's terror in the name of virtue. "Order" is a "true requirement of the soul," writes Simone Weil; she is thinking about the personal authority exercised by de Gaulle. She suggested legitimizing this authority with the aid of a plebiscite. Regardless of the intention, this proved to be the formula for modern dictatorship. The statements about the trade unions revoke earlier theses. At one time Simone Weil faulted them for being primarily focused on wage demands, viewing this as contemptuous of plans for social reform. Yet now the trade unions were supposed to be nothing but a vested interest group controlled by the state. One recognizes in these ideas notions about the primacy of the state that were propagandized by authoritarian circles before the war. In spite of her good intentions, we must consider Simone Weil's concept of a free society a failure. She attributed social grievances to one single source. In addition, she believed that she detected the cure in one single principle which united the social and the divine. It is horrifying that even literature was supposed to be delivered into the hands of the censor in order to adapt it to the norms of prescribed "morality." Here too, a ban on parties is pledged while various trends in art, like Cubism and Surrealism, are characterized as parties. In this way it was supposed to be possible, with the help of this one single principle, to hold society in check. She also adopted the slogans of the Pétain government which indicated that the writers too were to blame for France's downfall. André Gide fell under suspicion as did the principle of *l'art pour l'art*. This model for society is less reminiscent of freedom than it is of the force of authoritarian control.

In her last comprehensive paper, Simone Weil emphasizes her distance from Christianity: "Thus, with the exception of a few places from which a true light radiates, Christianity is a mere formality serving the interests of those who exploit the people."[180] Mysticism alone preserved the "true spirit of Christianity" Beyond pure mysticism however, "Roman idolatry has tainted everything."[181]

We must view this as Simone Weil's last word about religion, it posits a strict opposition to all efforts at accommodation in any direction. Paradoxes mark this text which contains the great next to the small, the far-sighted next to the short-sighted, and the progressive next to the antiquated.

A sentence like the following seems to contradict the other statements: "We only know, in general, that everything that happens, without exception, is according to the will of God."[182] From this resulted the conclusion that evil, rooted in divine will, is legitimate in the world and invincible as long as it corresponds to that will. Here we encounter the main essence of negative theology which dooms all attempts at reform to failure. Between fate and freedom, an unreconcilable contradiction stands out clearly. "Being firmly rooted is perhaps the most important and most misunderstood requirement of the human soul," reads Simone Weil's basic thesis.[183]

Yet the rigid model, which postulated the supremacy of evil, condemned every attempt at improvement to failure. She correctly diagnosed the problem of the cultural and moral disorientation and rootlessness of modern man. A few of her suggestions about solutions are still worth considering today. Indeed, in view of the progression of the problem of rootlessness, her suggestions have gained in importance. Nonetheless, the attempt to realize a free society with the help of authoritarian methods was in itself too contradictory to be considered anything other than a useless relic.

11

MIXED MESSAGE

Simone Weil is fascinating even when one does not share her ideas—which is frequently the case. After the Second World War her fame grew, her work was understood as an answer to the horrors which had been experienced. Intellectuals from numerous countries included her among the most exciting thinkers. For example, she exercised significant influence on Albert Camus and on Dwight Macdonald's New York journal, *Politics*. Religious circles, in turn, felt themselves particularly impacted by her theological reflections. What attracted many—apart from the message conveyed—was the life of this philosopher, the consistency, sincerity, self-sacrifice, which she had demonstrated.

In an article published in 1963, Susan Sontag explained her fascination with Simone Weil the person, not with the objective truth of Weil's work. This is contradicted by Sontag's assertion that the philosopher's influence rests on her extremely personal message: "We measure truth by the price of the suffering which the writer has paid—not according to the standard of an objective truth to which the writer's words correspond. Each of our truths must have its martyr."[184] Simone Weil belonged to those authors who made an impression not "by their intellectual passion, but by their instinct for the shrill, personal and spiritual extreme." According to Sontag, she stands with Kleist, Kierkegaard, Nietzsche, Dostoevsky, Baudelaire and Kafka, who emphasized "the morbid, the hysterical."

However, contrary to this explanation, offered in the spirit of romantic subjectivity, the writers cited did not attain importance as mere suffering martyrs. They were more. Had they done nothing but express their subjectivity, they would not have achieved their paramount significance. This significance is based precisely on the fact that their personal experiences were made universal. The "morbid" in Kleist, Kierkegaard or Kafka is as much the problem of each of them as it is of other human beings. The same holds true for Simone Weil. In this sense, T.S. Eliot once expressed the opinion that meaningful poets succeeded in transforming "their own personal pain into something rich and memorable, something universal and beyond personal." Susan Sontag's interpretation on the other hand, happily fixated on the fascination, decides in favor of the emotional drama to the detriment of the intellectual content.

In each of the authors mentioned, there is a spiritual substance which determines the actual value of the works. Although Susan Sontag praises Simone Weil as an aesthete— though she was not that, nor did she want to be—at the same time she sneers at "this woman's ridiculous political gestures, her conscious self-abnegation, her indefatigable reverence for suffering." Never would one wish for anyone to lead "such a life, to equal her in this devotion to martyrdom." Rejection of the intellectual content follows the aesthetic praise. A greater disrespect to a writer is hardly imaginable. It is the opposite of that which is wanted, namely, to be taken seriously.

Naturally, no one can imitate Simone Weil's life, or anyone else's, and no one in his right mind would give such foolish advice. Her gestures and thoughts carried the stamp of her personality, to that extent, they cannot be repeated. Yet that does not mean that they are entirely removed from others or that they have no value for others. Nor does it mean that it is impossible to extract some passages from her work to preserve and put to use. For this reason we do not limit ourselves, after Susan Sontag's example, to admiring the "martyrdom" of this philosopher. Instead, we ask what intellectual meaning her work might convey to us.

At the outset, we formulated the thesis that her work, notwithstanding the existing disparities, is tied together by common trends. Yet despite the ideas which unite the whole of her work, individual passages distinguish themselves with their special features. Two large phases stand out: the social-revolutionary years, which come to an end in 1937, and the subsequent religious phase of the last years of her life. I am unable to share Dorothee Sélle's view that such demarcations are unfounded.[185] Notwithstanding the unifying ideas, each stage, the revolutionary as well as the religious, has its own intellectual focal point with specific scope and perspectives. Also, within both of these stages of her life, distinctions exist which are worth noting. Differentiation is necessary.

In the area of social criticism, the anarchistic impetus was obsolete. The protest against politics, parties and the parliamentary system simply ignored the mechanisms of modern society and, thereby, condemned itself to powerlessness. Moreover, in the era of fascism, the anarchistic conception occasionally, though unintentionally, assisted reactionary aims. Out-moded too, is the cult of the proletariat, the image of the morally noble oppressed whose revolt was destined to create a better world.

However, by 1934 Simone Weil overcame these high-minded, naive notions dating from that early phase, when she emphatically stressed the inability of the workers to carry out an act of liberation. The "historical mission" of the working class, proclaimed by Marxists and anarchists, was called into question. With this, she demonstrated an astonishing ability for self-criticism, as well as a rare ability to stand alone and fight for her position. Because she had touched on venerable theses, which had been advanced for several generations, the uproar against this iconoclast was extremely embittered. This, of course, was something she could not change. She deduced her opinions from historical experience. Later decades provided validation of her views so that we today, more than ever, must assess the thesis of the "historical mission of the working class" as spurious.

The same holds true for her criticism of Marxism, it's Hegelian heritage was shrewdly recognized and rejected. "The entire doctrine, on which the conception of the Marxist revolution is based, lacks all scientific character."[186] This sentence, written more than a half-century ago, conveys indisputable truth even today. Marx encountered criticism because he had subscribed to "the cult of production, the cult of large-scale industry and a blind faith in progress."[187] The reproach was aimed at the fact that Marx had not wanted to overcome capitalism, but rather to improve upon it. On the tracks of capitalism, he had "transformed the powers of production into the deity of a religion." Thus Marxism was "the highest intellectual expression of bourgeois society."

Criticism was directed against unhampered production, its squandering of human labor and natural raw materials with the consequences of "disorder and waste." Simone Weil had the "emancipation of human beings" as her aim and this was something other than the "emancipation of the powers of production," to which Marx aspired. Averse to every eschatological vision of history, her thoughts were centered on the individual, on his existence, his suffering, his happiness. The individual should not be reduced to an object in the technological utopia. This criticism applied to private as well as state-controlled economic systems, liberal capitalism as well as authoritarian socialism. The conclusion inescapably ensued: the Soviet state was not a regime of social emancipation. Today this is generally recognized; the Gorbachov era documents this forcefully. However, in the thirties, such ideas were considered distinctly heretical.

In the same way, her shrewdness revealed the phenomena of spreading bureaucratic power. Certainly this was less original. Max Weber had already seen this as a feature of developed industrial society. "The bureaucracy belongs to the future," he had proclaimed.[188] Yet Weber warned against interpreting this phenomenon too one-sidedly and narrowly. Consequently, he was given to think, "that the bureaucracy, purely in and of itself, is an instrument of precision which can place itself at the disposal of various powerful special interests, the purely political, the purely economic, as well as any other."[189]

It can hardly be assumed that Simone Weil knew the writings of this German sociologist which, at the time, had received little attention in France. Her analyses of complete bureaucratic control were too generalized. Consequently, from these came a generalization which included systems as different as National Socialism, Stalinism and Roosevelt's New Deal.

Indeed, any abstraction which disregards important differences, is, at best, only partially helpful. That the Marxist workers' movement reproduced capitalism more than it prevailed over it, is a perception whose importance is visible to its full extent today. This is particularly true for the trade unions, which limited themselves to the selling of their product, the labor force, and basically turned their backs on social reforms. Thus they became protagonists of the capitalistic system whose collapse they once espoused. Simone Weil rebelled against "the devaluation of high idealism, of the almost aristocratic spirit of the socialist groups of the nineteenth century. This devaluation has brought about nothing but the degradation of the working class..."[190]

Of course, no one would be so deluded as to look for a complete program for social-political transformation in her texts. The great differences between the present and the 1930's precludes such a belief. Moreover, her work is far from systematic, rather it is a collection of fragments, beginnings and sketches. Some of these convey views worth considering. Others are questionable, full of contradictions, or even dubious. Simone Weil's work does not want to be consumed, but rather reflected upon. In keeping with her own critical substance, it desires a critical effort, apart from aesthetic and cult-like favor. Her ideas about ecology, decentralization, and the connection between physical and intellectual work were before their time and are of the highest quality.

The strength of this intellect was the abstraction, the extreme consistency. This often led to great discoveries, though sometimes it let differentiations, nuances, and temporal realities go unrecognized. This was the drawback of Weil's work. That society is composed of a multitude of groups, interests and ideas which no magic spell is able to charm—this reality of a pluralistic system did not come under her consideration. The absolute juxtaposition of good and evil, influenced by Plato, and later intensified by anarchistic ideology, ruled out an awareness of the fragmentariness of society. Consequently, authoritarian designs resulted. As the embodiment of good, the state is supposed to rule absolutely. The principle of distribution of power, a system of reciprocal controls for the resolution of conflicts, all of this was considered with contempt and was seen as unworthy of reflection. Simone Weil herself, this critic of totalitarianism, remained rooted in totalitarian thinking.

As a religious thinker, she also denied herself the appropriation of the familiar. Not belonging to any particular creed or church, her concept consists of elements from numerous doctrines—neo-platonism, Christianity, Judaism, Buddhism, gnosticism and the teachings of the Catharists. As a result, she believed that no intercession by a hierarchy of priests was required. He who believes is brought alone, face to face with God, as is always the case with mysticism. As an opponent of authoritarian organization, she sought the substance of all religions, the universal message, not that which was divisive and ordained by institutions. This, too, was a pioneering achievement. There are presently numerous efforts to overcome the divergences between religions in favor of the creation of a universal one. Consequently, Buddhism has a growing attraction for Christians, primarily on the strength of its spirit of tolerance of other religions, a spirit with which other religions are, for the most part, not acquainted.

As an individualist, Simone Weil is not suited to being a group idol. No saint and no cult figure, she was aware of the tragedy of her epoch with unequalled acuteness, and she grappled with problems which, essentially, are also our own. To identify oneself with her completely is impossible; in everything she was personal, independent and absolute. This generates distance, but there is also closeness, communication. Simultaneously distant and close, this striving philosopher, this sensitive thinker, so acutely aware of the historical tragedy, is our comrade. We are in a challenging dialogue with her thoughts—a dialogue which does not rest, which continuously poses new questions and does not end in the quietness of trite certainties.

In her stubborn consistency, Simone Weil arrived at great perceptions as well as grave misunderstandings. It is vital to distinguish carefully the one from the other. Exemplary is the unique courage of conviction, quite irrespective of her views which she changed often. The sharpness of her analytical mind was illuminating, exposing realities, trends, as well as misunderstandings which frighten one away. What she urged and, in a variety of ways, endeavored to realize, was the model for justice. When she turned her back on the world, seeking release in her encounter with God, she had to be alone in that void and withdraw herself from other human beings.

Jean Améry, who treated all of this with contempt, gave evidence of rare blindness. Is this only supposed to be subject matter for world-weary super intellectuals? This is a surprising misjudgment on the part of an author who embodied this type of intellectual like no other. In order to acquit himself with this case more easily, Améry sought to relegate it to the category of a "patient history." Of course, it is not irrelevant to consider Simone Weil's physical and psychological dispositions. It is as relevant here as for any other person. Yet this expert judgement presupposes precise data, which one should utilize with caution, in order to prevent being lead astray by all too rash conclusions. On this point, obviously, physicians and psychoanalysts have the last word.

If one tries to describe first impressions of her, a powerful self-confidence comes to mind, this was distinctive from early childhood and inclined her toward seeking untried paths. Striking also, are her ambivalent feelings toward her parents and her brother, in which love and indignation, affection and resistance flow into one another. Not to be overlooked are the headaches which started when she was twelve-years-old and continued with increasing intensity throughout her entire life. The rejection of femininity and the emphasis on masculine behavior deserves particular attention. Indeed, this was also an expression of her determination to be independent, as well as an expression of her movement from self-confidence to authoritarianism. Simone Weil lived within the intellectual. Disdaining the body and avoiding the sexual, she was frightened away by physical contact.

The American psychiatrist Robert Codes has dedicated a sympathetic, cautiously analytical, study to Simone Weil. There he writes: "It seems that she was not very concerned with her clothing and, in general, hardly took care of her body. Such behavior evidently appeased an inner voice and, to a considerable extent, satisfied her tendency to be autocratic. How she managed to be stronger than all of these impulses and desires of her body will always remain unknown to us as these are urges which we go through life partly enjoying, partly overcoming." Codes refers to "an astonishing discrepancy between Simone Weil's energetically demonstrated determination to be independent and her continued dependence on her parents, even in the fourth decade of her life."[191] Her psychology fed "her religious longings," Codes notes. Indeed, this could also be said about her revolutionary activity. "I believe one can positively say that she was in love with Jesus," he writes. "He became her lover; she accepted him in her mind and in her heart...She was something like a nun who followed her calling alone. She was an ambitious, devoted believer, desirous of encountering Him— perhaps even of becoming one of his saints."[192] This is only applicable in a limited way. Actually, she was far too much of a non-conformist to be a nun. Yet one must concur with Codes when he perceives "something stubbornly Protestant" about Simone Weil "in her wish to stand alone before God and to await the grace which was designated for her personally."[193] These are, indeed, features which hardly belong to Catholic worship.

Robert Codes, the physician, also discusses the issue of Simone Weil's eating, the aversion to eating which ultimately brought about her death. Medically, the diagnosis is anorexia, a mania for thinness beginning in puberty, whose causes are essentially psychological. Yet the author is very careful in the application of pathological concepts—exactly like Anna Freud, with whom he conducted numerous discussions about this case. Here Anna Freud refused to detect a sickness: "I do not think that we should characterize this case as clinical. Just read her essays and letters and try to imagine everything that penetrated her mind—it is no easy matter to ascertain this! We should try to see the world as she did, in order to fathom what she felt and said and why. She expressed herself lucidly and was strong-willed. If she is also supposed to have been sick —first in her head and later in her body—then we should indeed be careful in the naming of this sickness."[194]

The caution of this psychoanalyst differs from the careless estimations of Jean Améry and Susan Sontag. In her clinical practice, Anna Freud frequently had the opportunity to become involved with cases of anorexia. The refusal of nourishment was attributed to disturbances in the mother-child relationship. In the course of development, the child experiences "many negative emotional disturbances of anger, jealousy, and resentment toward the mother, which sometimes simply are displaced onto the mother."[195]

It is possible that this holds true for Simone Weil who was involved in a very close relationship with her mother, more intimate than with her father. Yet such a relationship did not rule out protest and resentment. In their book, *Les Indomptables*, the psychoanalysts Ginette Raimbault and Caroline Eliacheff describe the symptoms of anorexia which are also encountered in Simone Weil: "A will to self-sufficiency, to command of the body, of needs, and feelings; asceticism in terms of nourishment and sexuality, rejection of secondary sex characteristics...Appearing mostly in outwardly united families who correspond to our social norms, anorexia calls the family unit into question and exempts no one."[196] Affected above all are women from well-to-do environments, not always tragic heroines, "though tragedy is never missing from their lives..." Ginette Raimbault and Caroline Eliacheff refuse to characterize anorexia as a sickness. It is much more a question of probing a girl's attitude toward her "wishes, demands, and needs."[197]

This is the task we have put to ourselves here. Simone Weil's aura is unbroken. It is based on unusual abilities and behavior which vary from the commonplace, on an inexhaustible originality, and on a fearless determination to achieve results. Because she did not shrink from extreme conclusions, nothing was more unbearable to her than inconsequential, abstract, theorizing, careful probing for its own sake or for the sake of aesthetic charm. So rare was her awareness of the practical responsibility of thought that she wanted to decrease the gap between thought and action and prevail over the elite existence of the intellectuals. Therefore, there is her constant pursuit of experience: in society, in factory work, and in farm labor. Thought, like art, was alienated from life and should be called back to actual existence. As an isolated attempt this could not succeed, but the example remains. Whether the opposition of theory and practice can actually be eliminated is doubtful, yet conceivable is a convergence of the two spheres. Even if the goal was not attained, the attempt—to bring thought to bear on human problems—deserves admiration. The rule of an intellectual caste, with which Simone Weil also had become acquainted in the workers' movement, was supposed to come to an end. Still, in her theory of totalitarianism, a key position fell to the intellectuals as representatives of a new ruling class.

Conscious of the failure of this prospect, Simone Weil chose the destruction of thought as well as of practice—the destruction, quite simply, of life. The mystical experiment ultimately made Simone Weil into a solitary figure in the midst of an empty world. The basic impulse of her action and her theories was always of the moral type. Morality was at the root of all of her ideas, from beginning to end. Whatever the subject she wanted to address, the motives and goals were of the ethical type. Morality was supposed to take priority in society. The determination to carry out these ideas consistently caused unavoidable conflicts as well as her ultimate failure. In the era of such enormous crimes, she referred to the indestructible precept of morality. Accordingly, we have her exaggerated, but by no means absurd, reference to Antigone as a model for moral behavior against overwhelming state authority.

The conflict between morality and politics is an opposition of two principles, between heretics and lawgivers, between revolutionaries and rulers. In politics, compromise prevails. Development usually proceeds at a slow tempo, in so far as it does not actually stagnate. Quick accomplishments and absolute radical changes are rare. The moralist, on the other hand, is driven, is in a hurry, to secure immediate acceptance for his principles. Simone Weil embodies this type with an acuteness of her own. "Politics means a strong, slow drilling of hard boards." Nothing was more alien to her way of thinking than this sentence from Max Weber. She wanted to effect something quickly, more quickly than politics permitted. The moralist who avoids the complicated whirl of societal relationships refers to the iron laws of morality and looks beyond the daily occurrences to the eternal. This angers the politician who, at times justifiably, broaches the issues at hand in terms of its confounding details. However, often enough, he sinks in a desert of petty bureaucrats, short-sightedly failing to recognize the meaningful goals, which he still invokes, but only to pay lip service to them. There the admonitions of the moralist are required to call attention to principles which threaten to be lost during daily events.

Simone Weil's demand for total renewal could only be understood within the framework of a revolutionary plan. After its abandonment, the hope for radical change came to nothing. The only path to reform that remained was that of small steps which clearly require stamina and patience. This philosopher, who had only a sense for grandiose measures with an eschatological perspective, was not capable of this. Accordingly, there was her despair, the turning to religion, in which the mission of a radical transformation of humanity was taken up with a view to the theological.

In her last letters to her parents, written from the hospital, the dying Simone Weil writes that she is certain of possessing a "treasure of pure gold," which is to be conveyed. "But the experience, as well as the observation, of my contemporaries convince me more and more strongly that there is no one to receive it." This was of no consequence as in the near future, "the books and manuscripts of our epoch" will have "disappeared...This causes me no anguish. The gold mine is inexhaustible."[198]

As an author, she was always unpretentious. Indeed, for some time, she had thought in the completely different dimensions of eternity. On August 4, 1943, three weeks before her death, she designated Shakespeare's fools as ideal models. It was necessary to recognize their tragedy, beyond their comic demeanor: "The fools are the only people who speak the truth...Those in this world, who have reached the last degree of humiliation, far below beggary. They are not only without social standing, but also lacking in that which is valued most highly by everyone, reason—those people alone can speak the truth. All others lie."[199]

This was the last word from this visionary. It is also characteristic of the beginning of her highly individual career since Simone Weil always expressed that which she saw as the truth without diplomatic regard. In this sense, she was always the fool in the view of the establishment.

Leszek Kolakowski has characterized this as an opposition between priest and fool: "The priest is the guardian of the absolute. He serves the cult of the final, and of the acknowledged truisms which are rooted in the traditions. The fool is the doubter of everything which is considered self-evident"[200] Simone Weil was this doubter. She conveys an extraordinary attraction to thought. Yet she herself was often unfaithful to this task in that she sought a consistency which undermined the doubt. Again, in Kolakowski's words: "Total consistency is practically synonymous with fanaticism;

inconsistency is the source of tolerance."[201]

Such circumspection was alien to Simone Weil. In her thinking contrary tendencies collided, namely, the striving for absolute freedom and the search for a definitive solution to all contradictions through which the desire for freedom had to be overcome. The manichaistic opposition of good and evil, first in anarchistic, later in religious form, tended to demand an exclusiveness which undermined the principle of freedom. Only in solitude could she formulate her message which became completely extraneous. Nothing testifies to this more strongly than her last letters to her parents, from whom the mortally ill Simone Weil hid her true condition.

She died on August 24, 1943, according to the doctor's diagnosis, of "hunger and tuberculosis." On August 30th, the burial took place at Ashford cemetery in the English county of Kent. Eight people followed the coffin; there was no priest among them.

NOTES

1. R. Aron, *Mémoires,* Paris, 1983, p.78.
2. Jean Améry, *Simone Weil-Jenseits Der Legende,* in Merkur 1/1979.
3. J.M. Perrin and G. Thibon, *Simone Weil Telle Que Nous l'Avons Connue,* Paris, 1952, p.10.
4. A. Moulakis, *Simone Weil. Politik Der Askese,* Stuttgart, 1981, p. 23.
5. S. Pétrement, ed., *La Vie De Simone Weil I,* Paris, 1973, p.67.
6. S. Weil, *Attente De Dieu,* Paris, 1963, p.33-4.
7. S. Pétrement, *Weil I,* p.191.
8. Ibid., p.19.
9. *Die Schriften Der Anna Freud,* Band V, München, 1980, p.1436.
10. Cf. S. Pétrement, *Weil I,* p.68.
11. Ibid. p.69-70.
12. Cf. R. Aron, *Mémoires,* p.78.
13. S. deBeauvoir, *Memoiren Einer Tochter Aus Gutem Hause,* Reinbek, 1968, p.229.
14. P. Giniewski, *Simone Weil Ou La Haine De Soi,* Paris, 1978, p. 36-7.
15. G. Bally, ed., *Einführung In Die Psychoanalyse Sigmund Freud,* Reinbek, 1961, p.147.
16. Cf. P. Giniewski, p.55.
17. Cf. A. Moulakis, p.161.
18. R. Coles, *Simone Weil. A Modern Pilgrimage,* Reading, 1987, p.151.
19. M. Wicki-Vogt, *Jüdisches Denken In Geleugneter Tradition,* in:H.R. Schlette and A. Devaux, eds., Simone Weil. Philosophie, Religion, Politik, Frankfurt am Main, 1985, p.137-156.
20. Cf. S. Pétrement, *Weil I,* p.65.
21. Ibid., p.65-6.
22. Hannah Arendt, Rahel Varnhagen, München, 1959, p.186-211.
23. Alain, *Mars Oder Doe Psychologie Des Krieges,* Düsseldorf, 1983, p.77.
24. Cf. A. Moulakis, p.76.
25. A. Maurois, in: Alain, *Propos,* Paris, 1956, p.xiv.
26. G. Pascal, ed., *La Pensée d'Alain,* Paris, 1967, p.73.
27. Ibid., p.92.

28. Cf. Alain, *Propos,* p.549.
29. Cf. A. Moulakis, p.76.
30. Cf. Alain, *Propos,* p.1014.
31. Alain, *Las Passions Et La Sagesse,* Paris, 1960, p.333.
32. Cf. Alain, *Propos,* p.1039-41.
33. Cf. G. Pascal, p.175.
34. Ibid., p.181.
35. Ibid., p.196.
36. Cf. S. Pétrement, *Weil I,* p.65-6.
37. Ibid., p.96.
38. S. Weil, *Oeuvres Complétes I,* Paris, 1988, p.86.
39. Ibid., p.90.
40. Ibid., p.99-109
41. Cf. A. Moulakis, p.70.
42. S. Weil, *Oeuvres II,* Paris, 1988, p.59.
43. Ibid., p.71-5.
44. Ibid., p.67.
45. Ibid., p.45.
46. Ibid., p.76-7.
47. Ibid., p.95-7.
48. Ibid., p.233-35.
49. Ibid., p.90-l.
50. Ibid., p.395.
51. S. Weil, *Unterdrückung und Freiheit,* München, 1975/1987, p.33.
52. Ibid., p.62.
53. Ibid., p.36.
54. Ibid., p.102.
55. Cf. S. Pétrement, *Weil I,* p.279.
56. Cf. S. Weil, *Unterdrückung,* p.60.
57. Ibid., p.78.
58. K. Marx and F. Engels, *Ausgewählte Schriften I,* Stuttgart, 1953, p.35.
59. Cf. S. Weil, *Unterdrückung,* p.113-137.
60. A. Gorz, *Abschied vom Proletariat,* Frankfurt am Main, 1980, p.29, 31-2.
61. Cf. S. Weil, *Unterdrückung,* p.151-240.
62. Ibid., p.167.
63. M. Horkheimer and T. W. Adorno, *Dialektik Der Aufklärung,* Amsterdam, 1947, p.145, 13.
64. Cf. S. Weil, *Unterdrückung,* p.177.
65. Cf. M. Horkheimer and T. W. Adorno, p.19.
66. S. Weil, *La Source Grecque,* Paris, 1953, p.11.
67. Cf. S. Weil, *Unterdrückung,* p.231.
68. Ibid., p.240.

69. Ibid., p.232.
70. Ibid., p.235.
71. Ibid., p.202.
72. Cf. S. Weil, *Oeuvres II,* p.320-1.
73. S. Weil, Ecrits *Historiquest Et Politiques,* Paris, 1960, p.220.
74. S. Weil, *Fabriktagebuch Und Andere Schriften Zum Industriesystem,* Frankfurt am Main, 1978, p.25.
75. Ibid., p.50-l.
76. Ibid., p.61.
77. Ibid., p.123.
78. Ibid., p.39.
79. Ibid., p.31.
80. Ibid., p.24.
81. Ibid., p.40.
82. Cf. S. Pétrement, *Weil II,* p.53.
83. Ibid., p.58.
84. Cf. S. Weil, *Fabriktagebuch,* p.140-77.
85. Ibid., p.186.
86. Ibid., p.191.
87. Ibid., p.213-222.
88. Cf. S. Weil, *Ecrits,* p.209-216.
89. Ibid., p.220-224.
90. Ibid., p.392-3.
91. Cf. S. Weil, *La Source,* p.42.
92. Ibid., p.32.
93. S. Weil, *Oppression Et Liberté,* Paris, 1955, p.213.
94. Cf. S. Weil, *Ecrits,* p.231.
95. Ibid., p.237.
96. Ibid., p.243.
97. Ibid., p.242.
98. Ibid., p.246.
99. Ibid., p.249.
100. Ibid., p.251.
101. Ibid., p.254-5.
102. Ibid., p.275.
103. Ibid., p.276.
104. Ibid., p.286.
105. Ibid., p.296-312.
106. Cf. S. Pétrement, *Weil II,* p.235-6.
107. Cf. S. Weil, *Ecrits,* p.341.
108. Ibid., p.363.
109. Ibid., p.315.
110. W. Weil, *La Connaissance Surnaturelle,* Paris, 1950, p.317.

111. A. Krogmann, ed., *Simone Weil,* Reinbek, 1970, p.45.
112. S. Weil, *Schwerkraft Und Gnade,* München, 1989, p.204, 201.
113. Ibid., p.204.
114. Ibid., p.205-6.
115. S. Weil, *Attente De Dieu,* Paris, 1963, p.37.
116. Cf. S. Weil, *La Connaissance,* p.9-10.
117. Ibid., p.129.
118. Cf. S. Weil, *Attente,* p.43.
119. Ibid., p.43-44.
120. Ibid., p.49.
121. Ibid., p.50.
122. Ibid., p.31.
123. Ibid., p.45.
124. Ibid., p.65.
125. Ibid., p.66.
126. Ibid., p.66-7.
127. Ibid., p.68.
128. S. Weil, *Cahiers II,* Paris, 1953, p.207.
129. S. Weil, *Intuitions Pré-Chrétiennes,* Paris, 1951, p.158.
130. Cf. S. Weil, *Attente,* p.119.
131. Ibid., p.120.
132. Cf. S. Weil, *Ecrits,* p.69.
133. Ibid., p.120.
134. Ibid., p.70-71.
135. Ibid., p.74.
136. Ibid., p.74.
137. Cf. S. Weil, *Schwerkraft,* p.233.
138. J. Cabaud, ed., *Simone Weil. Die Logik Der Liebe,* Freiburg- München, 1968, p.284.
139. Ibid., p.284-5.
140. Ibid., p.283.
141. Cf. S. Pétrement, *Weil II,* p.390.
142. Cf. J. Cabaud, ed., *Simone Weil,* p.278.
143. Cf. S. Pétrement, *Weil II,* p.294.
144. Ibid., p.297.
145. Cf. J. Cabaud, *Simone Weil,* p.271.
146. Cf. S. Pétrement, *Weil I,* p.308.
147. Cf. J. Cabaud, *Simone Weil,* p.280
148. S. Weil, *La Pensanteur El La Grâce,* Paris, 1963, p.167.
149. Cf. S. Weil, *La Connaissance,* p.223.
150. Cf. S. Weil, *Attente De Dieu,* p.33.
151. Ibid., p.27.
152. Cf. Simone Weil, *Cahiers II,* p.394.

153. Ibid., p.241.
154. Ibid., p.413.
155. Cf. S. Weil, *Schwerkraft,* p.24.
156. Ibid., p.25.
157. Ibid., p.156-7.
158. Ibid., p.133.
159. Ibid., p.151.
160. W. Nigg, *Große Heilige,* Zürich, 1968, p.281, 278.
161. G. Scholem, *Über Einige Grundbegriffe Des Judenturms,* Frankfurt am Main, 1970, p.75.
162. Cf. S. Weil, *Schwerkraft,* p.11-12.
163. K. Jaspers, *Der Philosophische Glaube,* Frankfurt am Main- Hamburg, 1960, p.43-4.
164. Cf. S. Weil, *Schwerkraft,* p.27.
165. S. Weil, *Venise Sauvée,* Paris, p.25.
166. Ibid., p.67.
167. Ibid., p.15.
168. Ibid., p.16.
169. S. Weil, *Ecrits de Londres Et Derniéres Lettres,* Paris, 1957, p.185-215.
170. Ibid., p.98-108.
171. Ibid., p.123.
172. Ibid., p.124.
173. Ibid., p.74-84.
174. S. Weil, *Die Einwurzelung,* Münxhwn, 1956, p.11.
175. Ibid., p.77.
176. Ibid., p.80.
177. Ibid., p.351.
178. Ibid., p.94.
179. Ibid., p.96.
180. Ibid., p.360.
181. Ibid., p.403.
182. Ibid., p.387.
183. Ibid., p.71.
184. S. Sontag, *Kunst Und Antikunst,* Frankfurt am Main, 1982, p.102.
185. Dorothee Sölle, *Die Aktualität, Simone Weil,* in: Merkur 3/1979.
186. Cf. S. Weil, *Unterdrückung,* p.158.
187. Ibid., p.266.
188. M. Weber, *Wirtschaft Und Gesellschaft,* Tübingen, 1976, p.834.
189. Ibid., p.25.
190. Cf. S. Weil, *Unterdrückung,* p.273.
191. Cf. R. Coles, *Simone Weil. A Modern Pilgrmage,* p.118.
192. Ibid., p.25.
193. Ibid., p.119.

194. Ibid., p.150.
195. Ibid., p.28.
196. Cf. *Die Schriften Der Anna Freud,* Bank V. p.1436.
197. G. Raimbault and C. Eliacheff, *Les Indomptables,* Paris, 1989, p.69.
198. Ibid., p.267.
199. Cf. S. Weil, *Ecrits,* p.250-51.
200. Ibid., p.255.
201. L. Kolakowski, *Der Mensch Ohne Alternative,* München, 1960.
202. Ibid., p.240.

SELECTED BIBLIOGRAPHY

WORKS BY SIMONE WEIL IN FRENCH

La Pesanteur Et La Grâce, (Paris, 1948)

Attente De Dieu, (Paris, 1948)

L'Enracinement, (Paris, 1949)

La Conaissance Surnaturelle, (Paris, 1950)

La Condition Ouvrière, (Paris, 1951)

Intuitions Pré-Chrétiennes, (Paris, 1951)

Lettre À Un Religieux (Paris, 1951)

Cahiers I - III, (Paris, 1951-56)

La Source Grecque, (Paris, 1953)

Oppression Et Liberté, (Paris, 1955)

Venise Sauvée, (Paris, 1955)

Ecrits De Londres Et Dernières Lettres, (Paris, 1957)

Ecrits Historiques Et Politiques, (Paris, 1960)

Pensées Sans Ordre Concernant L'Amour De Dieu, (Paris, 1962)

Essais, Lettres Et Fragments, (Paris, 1965)

Poèmes, Suivis de Venise Sauvée, (Paris, 1968)

Many of her efforts appear in the collected edition of 16 volumes, edited by André A. Devaux and Florence de Lussy:

> *Premiers Écrits Philosophiques*, (Paris, 1988)
> *Ecrits Historiques Et Politiques*, (Paris, 1988)

WORKS BY SIMONE WEIL IN ENGLISH

Gravity and Grace. Introduced by Gustave Thibon. Translated by Emma Crawford. Routledge & K. Paul. London, 1952.

Intimations of Christianity Among the Ancient Greeks. Edited and translated by Elizabeth Chase Geissbulher. Routledge & K. Paul. London, 1957.

Notebooks. Translated by Arthur Wills. Putnam's Sons. New York, 1956.

Oppression and Liberty. Introduction by F.C. Ellert. Translated by Arthur Wills and John Petire. Univ. of Mass. Press. Amherst, 1973.

Selected Essays, 1934-43. Translated by Richard Rees. Oxford Univ. Press. London, 1962.

Seventy Letters. Translated by Richard Rees. Oxford Univ. Press. London, 1965.

Simone Weil: An Anthology. Edited and introduced by Sian Miles. Weidenfeld & Nicolson. New York, 1986.

Simone Weil 1909-1943, Selections. Edited and translated by Dorothy Tuck McFarland and Wilhelmina Van Ness. Univ. of Mass. Press. Amerherst, 1987.

The Iliad or the Poem of Force. Translated by Mary McCarthy. Pendle Hill. Wallingford, Pa., 1956.

Waiting for God. Introduction by Leslie Fiedler. Translated by Emma Groufurd. Harper & Row. New York, 1973.

SELECTED WORKS ABOUT SIMONE WEIL IN ENGLISH

Allen, Diogenes, *Three Outsiders: Pascal, Kierkegaard, Simone Weil.* Crowley Publications. Cambridge, Mass., 1983.

Cabaud, Jacques, *Simone Weil: A Fellowship in Love.* Channel Presses. 1965.

Coles, Robert, *Simone Weil, A Modern Pilgrimage.* Addison-Wesley. Reading, Mass., 1987.

Davy, Marie Madelaine, *The Mystique of Simone Weil.* Beacon Press. Boston, 1951.

Hellman, John. *Simone Weil: An Introduction to her Thought.* Fortress Press. 1984.

McLellan, David. *Utopian Pessimist: The Life & Thought of Simone Weil.* Poseidan Press. New York, 1990.

Nevin, Thomas. *Simone Weil: Portrait of a Self-Exiled Jew.* University of North Carolina Press. 1991.

Pétrement, Simone. *Simone Weil: A Life.* Translated by Raymond Rosenthal. Pantheon Books. New York, 1976.

Rees, Richard. *A Study of D.H. Lawrence and Simone Weil.* University of S. Ill. Press. Carbondale, 1959.

Tomlin, Eric Walter. *Simone Weil.* Bowes and Bowes. Cambridge, 1954.

CHRONOLOGY TABLE

1909   Born Simone Weil on February 3 in Paris. Her father, Bernard Weil, comes from Alsace and is a physician. Her mother, Salomea Weil, née Reinherz, was born in Russia. The Weils, a Jewish family, are not religious; she is raised in a liberal home atmosphere.

1925   Baccalaureate in Philosophy. Pupil of Alain at the Lycée Henri IV.

1928   Accepted into L'Ecole Normale Supérieure.

1929   Publications in Alain's journal, *Libres Propos*.

1931   Simone Weil signs, next to Sartre, Romain Roland and others, a protest against the obligatory officer's career for the "Normaliens". She passes the "Agrégation", the State Examination for teaching in high schools and becomes a philosophy teacher at a girls' school in Le Puy. Trade union activity, participation in workers' demonstrations.

1932   Residence in Germany. Wrote series of articles about the political climate. Disciplinary transfer to Auxerre.

1933   At union congresses, her criticism of the Communist Internationale causes a sensation. Publication of the essay, "Prospects: Are We Heading for a Proletarian Revolution?" Conversations with Trotsky.

1934   Formulation of the composition, "Reflections on the Causes of Freedom and Social Oppression." December: Temporary worker in the factory, Elektro-Firma Alshom.

1935   Ear infections and migraines, vacation in Switzerland. June 5–August 22: Machinist at Renault, then vacation in Spain and Portugal. October: Teacher at the Lycée in Bourges. Interest in Gregorian music, attends early mass.

1936   Declares pacifism, rejects military resistance to Germany. Shows support for the strikes in France. August 8: Simone Weil travels to Barcelona to be a volunteer in the Spanish Civil War. She becomes a member of the anarchistic military and is burned by boiling oil while cooking. Returns with her parents to France.

1937   Vacation in Italy. Publication of Essays. Teacher at the Lycée in Saint-Quentin.

1938   Mystical ecstacy during Holy Week at the Benedictine Abbey, Solesmes.

1939   Revision of pacifistic view.

1940   Develops plan for the creation of a troop of nurses. Lectures on the Indian epic Bhagavadgita, studies Sanskrit. When German attack on France begins she flees from Paris with her parents. In Vichy, Simone Weil works on the tragedy, Venise Sauvee. September 15: Arrival in Marseille. Collaboration on the journals, Cahiers du Sud and Cahiers du Témoignage Chrétien. Encounter with the Dominican Prior Jean-Marie Perrin. October: Letter to Ministry of Education to protest against her dismissal from the teaching profession because of anti-Jewish laws.

1941   Formulation of Cahiers begins. Participation in discussions in the crypt of the Dominican convent in Marseille. August: Agricultural work on Gustave Thibons' farm. September–October: Letter to the Commissioner for Jewish Questions to demand reinstatement in the teaching profession.

1942   Formulation of religious texts. Farewell letter to Pater Perrin. May 14: Departure for Algeria with her parents. July 6: Arrival in New York. November 10: Passage to England.

1943   Involvement in the Resistance; her plan, to be sent to France for sabotage purposes, is rejected. Simone Weil writes *Taking Root* and fasts to the point of physical collapse. April 15: Admitted to Middlesex Hospital. August 17: Transferred to Grosvenor Sanatorium in Ashford-Kent. August 24: Death due to undernourishment. August 30: Burial in the New Cemetery in Ashford.

Heinz Abosch, (b. 1918) Emigrated from his native Germany to France in 1933 to study art. In 1945 he became a newspaper correspondent in Paris and in 1956 a publicist in West Germany. His book publications include an introduction to the work of Leo Trotsky, *Trotski zur Einführung.* He is also the editor of Simone Weil's, *Unterdrückung und Freiheit* (Oppression and Freedom), *Fabriktagebuch* (Factory Journal), and of Alain's *Mars oder die Psychologie des Krieges (Mars, or the Psychology of War.)*